BORN TO BE BLESSED

7 Keys to Joyful Living

by

Judy McCoy Carman, M.A.

Foreword by Ann Nunley, M.F.A.
Author of *Inner Counselor*

SeaShore

Pittsburgh, PA

ISBN 1-58501-005-7

Trade Paperback
© Copyright 1999 Judy McCoy Carman, M.A.
Web site: www.cjnetworks.com/~jcarm
E-mail: jcarm@cjnetworks.com
All rights reserved
First Printing—1999
Library of Congress #98-88530

Request for information should be addressed to:

CeShore Publishing Co.
The Sterling Building
440 Friday Road
Pittsburgh, PA 15209
www.CeShore.com

Cover design: Michelle Vennare - CeShore
Typesetting: Drawing Board Studios
CeShore is an imprint of SterlingHouse Publisher, Inc.

The author of this book does not dispense medical advice or prescribe the use of any technique as a form of treatment for physical or mental problems without the advice of a physician either directly or indirectly. In the event you use any of the information in this book for such treatment, neither the author nor the publisher can assume any responsibility for your actions. The intent of the author is only to offer general information which may assist you in personal growth.

Printed in Canada

This book is all about you:
The mystery of you,
The miracle of you.

You are beautiful and bright.
You are a miracle of light.

There is awesome power
within you; infinite beauty;
divinity overflowing.

You are seven-times blessed
by the Creator of All-That-Is,
loved, cherished, and adored.

Dedicated:
To my children who give me endless joy,
And to the children of the world.
May they inherit from us peace, faith,
joy, love, and a sense of the Sacred in
themselves and All-That-Is.

Contents

Acknowledgments

Inspiration for this book came from my many clients over the years who shared their hearts and healing with me; from my experiences living and camping in the wilderness that I love; from the many animals, human and otherwise, who have loved me and touched my life; from Jesus and my guardian angels who are always comforting me; from the mystics and shamans of many faiths who have shared their wisdom and ecstasy; from the courageous environmentalists, animal protectionists, and peace and justice workers who will not give up hope; from my personal challenges that led me out of atheism into God's loving arms; from the Wolf Women and the intrepid Friday Group; from my parents and family who specialize in questioning authority and creating beauty; from the priceless treasure of my motherhood; and from my search for my beloved daughter, Judy, whose first letter to me arrived on the day I finished this manuscript.

Thanks and blessings to all who helped specifically with the book: Neil Shelton and Kevin Gunn for computer therapy and assistance; Ann Nunley for writing the foreword and giving me loving encouragement and advice; Anna McCoy and Missy McCoy Fortel, my amazing sisters, for their artistic assistance; Cynthia Sterling, Michelle Burton-Brown, and the staff at SterlingHouse Publishers for believing in me; and Michael Carman, my husband, for his steadfast devotion. Thanks also to: Joyce Berman, Kent Deeds, Vicki Douglas, Anna Franke, James Dillet Freeman, Jackie Giuliano, Ph.D., Roberta Houseman, Ph.D., A.J. LoScalzo, Caz Loth, Priscilla McKinney, Ph.D., Victoria Moran, Bob Nunley, Ph.D., Lynate Pettengill, Reverend Sherry Schultz, Reverend Sandy King Shipley, Louann Stahl, Rosemary Sweeney, R.N., Julie Vernon, and all my dear friends and family who have encouraged and helped with the writing of this book.

Foreword

You are a child of the Universe, you deserve to be here.
Desiderata

This beautiful statement truly captures the inspirational essence of *Born To Be Blessed*. Each of us who is aware of our own emotional struggles and who has served as friend, comforter, and counselor knows that the greatest obstacle to joy is the lack of self-worth that we each sometimes experience.

Having felt so often judged, we become our own most severe critic. Judging ourselves we, in turn, judge others and thus subject ourselves to endless downward spirals of inadequacy. Perhaps the most difficult reality to accept is the fact that, in spite of ourselves, we **are** accepted, we **are** intrinsically whole, and we **have** value. Someone once said, "If you find yourself separated from God, it is you who have moved." This lovely book is about finding one's way back to unity, love and intrinsic self-value.

Through self-judgment and our judgment of others we develop "selective" perception. For instance, if we read the Holy books of our religions through attitudes of unworthiness, we will focus on those passages that support the belief that God is an angry, judgmental and vengeful force. When we judge ourselves as unworthy, we tend to project angry and vengeful judgment upon others. This can be a form of protective deflection—"If 'they' are wrong, I must be 'right'!" Anger and judgment are always divisive, and can never provide a path to the Universal Unity of the Divine.

"Hell" and "evil" are synonyms for separation from the Divine. I am convinced that Hell is not a place we go to be punished after death. We are "in Hell" whenever we feel totally alone, separated from others and from God. Evil is based on ignorance of the interconnectedness of all things. When we truly grasp this interconnection and interdependence, we realize that we cannot do harm to another without harming ourselves. This separation and ignorance is not a punishment meted out by the Divine. We put ourselves in the place of separation called Hell, and we choose the blind ignorance that creates evil. However, having put ourselves there, we can always choose to take ourselves out.

In our search for Unity, we can choose paths that do not divide and separate. Faith and deep convictions are part of this journey. However, when our convictions are dependent upon specific religious and historical persuasions, divisions often occur. Each religious path has its historical foundation. But recorded history is subject to the interpretive fallacy of record and memory. Thus, what becomes more important than the interpreted historical record is the *Divine message* that is conveyed. When we look at the *message* of each of the major religions, we can find commonality and agreement. True spiritual wisdom is the same no matter its source. While it is wonderful to be part of a religious group in which we can share and experience our spiritual nature, we must guard against the potential within religious forms that separate us from others through judgment and divisive aggrandizement. We need to remember that whatever separates us from others also separates us from God, and that only by embracing our own self-worth, can we accept the worthiness of others.

Born To Be Blessed is ecumenical and universal. Its message reconnects us with a deep sense of belonging and inspires us to accept a true sense of our own worthiness and to be ever mindful of the beauty in all of life. This is not a book to be read once and then set aside. **It is a keepsake of inspirational thought and prayer to be enjoyed on a daily, ongoing basis.**

Ann Nunley, M.F.A.,
seminar leader, artist, and author of:
Inner Counselor: An Intuitive Guide for Life's Journey;
1998-99 Co-President of the International Society for
the Study of Subtle Energies and Energy Medicine

Introduction

TO BEGIN WITH

This book is in your hands:

>*To inspire you.*
>
>*To remind you of your greatness.*
>
>*To bring you joy.*
>
>*To prove how deeply you are loved.*
>
>*To give you a solid foundation for real and lasting high self-esteem.*
>
>*To give you hope for your future and for the future of the planet.*
>
>*To demonstrate that you are holy, and that all creation is sacred.*

In these pages you will find the keys to:

>*Who you really are.*
>
>*Why you are here on earth today.*
>
>*How you can live a life of joy and harmony.*
>
>*How you can fully love yourself and thereby cherish and love others.*
>
>*How you can co-create with God the life you want and deserve.*
>
>*How you can feel your intimate connection with all life.*
>
>*How your intimate connection with all life helps to heal you and the planet.*
>
>*How you can participate in the evolution of consciousness that is taking place on earth now and into the 21st century.*

Here you will find *the seven mystical blessings of the universe that prove the sacredness of all beings and the holiness of you.* Here you will find an inspirational guide for your journey to self-empowerment, love, healing, purpose, ecstasy, and oneness with all creation.

Many outstanding books explain the principles of manifesting health, wealth, and spiritual peace and joy. However, many of us are unable to make these great and universal principles work as well for us as we would like. The reason for this is clear. We are such powerful beings that we can actually prevent ourselves from receiving joy. Why would we do that? It is because at some place within us, we believe we are not worthy to receive the love and joy we long for. Both unconscious and conscious thoughts of unworthiness can cause us to sabotage even our best efforts at gaining the success and joy we want in our lives.

The book you hold in your hands explains what you must know first, before true joy can be yours. As you allow the words in this book to bless your body, your mind, and your soul, you will remember the truth of who you really are. I pray that, as this wisdom, which is already within you, is renewed within your heart and mind, you will be lifted up, inspired, and filled with the zest and joy for living that you so richly deserve.

SEVEN MESSAGES: THE COMMON THREAD OF ALL RELIGIONS

This book that you are holding is full of hope and full of bliss. This book carries seven basic messages from masters and mystics of ancient and modern times: Sufi mystics, Catholic saints, Zen masters, Native shamans, my own guru Jesus, and many other wise, awakened ones who have explored the frontiers of spiritual consciousness and come back with priceless treasure. And these messages come not just from religious teachers, but from other folks as well: people who have had near death experiences and angelic visitations, scientists on the frontiers of quantum physics and consciousness research, people who have experienced miraculous healings, and many others. These people who have tasted even one tiny drop of the nectar of Divine Love are repeating the same message to us over and over again. They are telling us that *we are all Heaven Itself, outrageous in our loveliness, and tremulously, tenderly, eternally adored.*

My quest for many years has been to find the common thread that runs through all religions, to find the similarities instead of the differences, and in that way glean something solid and comforting and universal; to give some shape to my faith. The spinners of that common thread are the smiling ones who have experienced God's presence firsthand, face to face, hand to hand.

As I studied the writings and poems and songs of these sweet sages, I discovered seven distinct, consistent, and clear messages which appeared again and again in sacred musings worldwide. It does not matter from what religions or cultures the messengers have come; the messages remain consistent and clear.

Once a being has felt the Tender Touch of the Great Creator, that one is changed forever and cannot keep still about it. The seven clear messages that I found are continually repeated tidings of Unconditional, Eternal Love. And these words are not just meant for the ears of the pious and ascetic. They are given to all of us. They are given to all that lives and moves and is. *They are our seven blessings, no matter who we are, no matter what we have done.*

I began this quest to save my own soul, and found along the pathway, that my soul was never lost; indeed that I was never lost. Rather have I discovered that I have been tenderly cherished and watched over always, as you have been.

WHO ARE YOU?

Sri Ramana, an illumined master of 20th century India, tells us to always be asking: "Who am I?" It is by asking this question at every turn: "Who am I?"; at every new event: "Who am I?"; at every disconsoling thought: "Who am I?"; at every lucky break: "Who am I?" It is in that asking that we go deeper and deeper into our souls until we remember who we really are. As we grow in spirit, we find to our amazement that we do not have to change who we are. What we must do is remember who we are, for who we are is cause for awe and wonder.

We are all much closer than we think to breathing in and living out our divinity. Our spiritual path is not a line or a ladder. It is instead very looped and spiraled, leading us ever within, ever within. It is in the depths of ourselves that we discover that the magical, mystical, holy being that we long to become is there within us waiting to be set free. Like the genie trapped in a bottle, that genie must be freed by the one who holds the bottle.

All that we are right now—with all the mistakes and grand deeds we've accomplished; all the heartaches and joys we've felt; and all the harm and healing we've done—is holy. Let us embrace ourselves, our *whole* selves, with all our faults and past errors, for it is in that embrace that we rub the magic lamp and set our bright spirits free.

All of us are glorious. All humans, all furry creatures, all those that swim, and those that fly, the stones, the mountains, the tiniest flowers—we are all pure love energy made manifest in colors and forms and wondrous voices. We are all holy beings walking together on holy ground.

THE MYSTERIOUS NUMBER SEVEN

The number seven is very mysterious. It shows up again and again in science and religion. It is considered by many to be the number of perfection. There are:

seven elementary colors in the visible spectrum
seven musical notes in each key
seven days in a week
seven Christian sacraments
seven days of creation
seven directions: east, west, north, south, up, down, and within
seven wonders of the world
seven continents on earth
seventh heaven: Mohammedanism's highest abode of bliss
seventy times seven: a key to forgiveness
seven chakras or energy centers in the body

And there are seven blessings.
You are seven times blessed. You are music; you are color; you are earth; you are heaven. You are a holy wonder of the world.

THE INVIGORATING POWER OF SELF-RESPECT

Without self-respect, we human beings have an uncanny ability to sabotage our best efforts at creating a good life on this earth. Because we are so powerful, our negative thoughts about ourselves can regularly create destructive circumstances in our lives. In order that we may consistently and authoritatively define and develop a better life for ourselves, our loved ones, and our world, we must find a way to love ourselves, believe in ourselves, and consider ourselves worthy of receiving and giving love, abundance, and joy.

The seven blessings from God, Goddess, Creator, Big Holy, the Great I Am, Great Spirit—these seven blessings belong to you. No one can take them away from you. They are the birthright of your soul, your divine inheritance. They are the building blocks, the foundation stones of your true identity. You are free to step up and stand upon them and proclaim the truth of who you are. Once claimed and fully owned by you, you can never again linger overlong in self-doubt and deprecation. Knowing who you are, in the core of your being; knowing the ecstasy the universe feels simply because you are here; you can build the life of your highest dreams.

I have recorded these blessings for you to read and feel and celebrate. May we all fall hopelessly in love with life, and with all creation, and with ourselves.

Imagine what wonders we shall set ablaze with such fiery love!

THE SEVEN MESSAGES ARE ALL BLESSINGS FOR YOU FROM GOD

In this book, I have synthesized the discoveries and the stories of physicists, psychologists, spiritual teachers, mothers and fathers, students and children, workers and dreamers into *The Seven Keys to Joyful Living.* These seven keys are keys to joy, because they explain to us who we really are and how much God loves us. They give us seven simple truths about ourselves that help us make sense out of life, find comfort in the midst of hardship, find clarity in the midst of confusion, and continue to grow in spiritual consciousness.

God has been speaking to us through all these people throughout the ages. The seven Divine messages come through them again and again. The tidings never change. And the good news is that each message, *each key is a glorious blessing for every single one of us. We were all, each one of us, without exception,* **BORN TO BE BLESSED.**

The blessings are clear and bold and true. On the next two pages, you will find a love letter to you from God. In that love letter you will find your seven keys to joy, the seven perennial truths, the seven recurring messages that God has given to people throughout the ages. In that love letter you will find *YOUR SEVEN BLESSINGS.*

It is for Love that you are here. Love rejoices that you have chosen to be here.

May your heart be light;
Your body be nourished;
And your soul find its wings
as you continue on your
Sacred Journey.

THE SEVEN BLESSINGS
A Love Letter to you
From God

My Beloved Child,

YOU ARE IMMORTAL. Your very existence is holy and eternal. Your own divinity is etched upon the universe forever. You will make transitions from this realm to others, but always you will live within Me and I within you as we dance and play together.

YOU BELONG. Without you, I would not be complete, nor would Life, nor Love. You are part of the One Divine Cosmic Family. Absolutely everyone and everything is connected in this great sea of Love. Without you We are not whole. You are needed and wanted and adored.

YOU ARE POWERFUL. I am the Power of Love. Your cells and your breathing, your thoughts and longings all vibrate with that Power. You breathe in my awesome Love for you and all Creation. You breathe out your electrifying Love for All-That-Is. You are Heaven brought to Earth.

YOU ARE LOVED. I love you without boundaries or limits. There is nothing as vast and infinite as My Love for you. There is nothing you can do that will dissuade Me from loving you. You are made of My Love and nothing can separate us from Each Other.

YOU ARE CREATIVE. Together you and I are Co-Creators. We birth energy into matter, light into form, Heaven into Earth, vibration into song. With every child you comfort, every stroke of your pen, every word from your lips and every kiss, you can fill the universe with more beauty, more mystery, and more Love.

YOU ARE PERFECT. When you feel lost, alone, different, or full of faults, remember that you are perfect to Me right now just as you are. I see only Exquisite Beauty and Elegance and Grace in you, Beloved. If the world seems to judge you or the path you have taken, remember there is no "right" path home to Me. You are already here in My arms this very day.

YOU ARE DIVINE. There is nothing in Heaven or Earth that is not Sacred and filled with Me. I am in All-That-Is, and All-That-Is lives and breathes in Me. I am Life, and I am Love. Your spirit sees Me looking back at you from every face, every drop of rain, every stone, every gust of wind. When you look in the mirror, you see your face and mine. There, in you, rejoices the Divine.

LOVE FOREVER, GOD

1st

BLESSING

YOU ARE ETERNAL

Your very existence is holy and eternal. Your own Divinity is etched upon the universe forever. You will make transitions from this realm to others, but always you will live within Me and I within You as We dance and play together.

The Blessing of Eternal Life

This is our first blessing. It belongs to you and me and everyone, no matter what our religion, philosophy, race, or species. All religions speak of it. Many people have experienced it firsthand in near-death experiences. Scientists are beginning to acknowledge it and are even attempting to explain it. This message is ancient and universal. It is very good old news.

> *The reality of my life cannot die, for*
> *I am indestructible consciousness.*
> —Paramahansa Yogananda, 20th century yogi

How special you are! You are "indestructible consciousness". You can never cease to be. You—the essence of you—is forever young, vibrant, alive, and living within the endless streaming of God's Love.

Now, during your visit to earth, you have added a physical body to who you are. You are a heavenly being made of light. You have literally brought heaven into visibility; you have brought heaven to earth.

Your uniqueness, the essence that is completely and utterly you, is so treasured in this universe and so loved that God cannot bear to lose you. And so—you will always be.

BEHOLDING YOUR BREATHTAKING BEAUTY

> *Friends of other lives easily recognize*
> *one another in the astral world.*
> *Rejoicing at the immortality of*
> *friendship, they realize the*
> *indestructibility of love, often doubted*
> *at the time of the sad, delusive*
> *partings of earthly life.*
> —Sri Yukteswar Giri, 19th century Hindu yogi,
> quoted by Paramahansa Yogananda

It is difficult sometimes to remember who we are. The world seems so finite when we are trying hard to make ends meet and feeling the stress of deadlines and complex, contradictory rules. Paramahansa Yogananda, a spiritual teacher from India, called those of us with family responsibilities "householders". He said there is no reason that we cannot be filled with the consciousness of our true nature, just because we are involved with the ways of the world. We do not have to be contemplative, celibate monks and nuns to see the truth of who we are.

Leave this time for a few moments and travel back in your mind to a magic place in your life. Perhaps, it was the moment you fell in love and beheld your lover in all his radiance close beside you, or the moment you first gazed into your baby's eyes. Or maybe you recall a time when you were in awe at your first sight of the sea or a glimpse of a rainbow or, perhaps, a puppy looking up at you as if you were king of the world. Hold that feeling you had of wonder at the exquisite beauty before you. Recall your feeling of awe and your sense that you were privileged to be witnessing something divine and heavenly. Thousands of songs, maybe millions, have been written about those magical enchantments when we see our earth angel or feel the starry vastness of our love for someone dear.

Now, filled with that feeling, gaze at yourself in a mirror and observe that same faint glow of perfection around you that you have seen in others. It is there. Believe me. You cannot see it if you look at your image in the usual manner; that is, with the old critical eye which wastes no time picking out all the physical imperfections of hair, skin, weight, and clothing. Look at your image instead with your spiritual eye, for that is how you looked at your beloved. If you cannot quite see the intense light and the nearly blinding beauty that you are, then, try this. Imagine what you must look like to God who loves you so much and cannot bear to be apart from you for even an instant.

*How wonderful is the wisdom in the
Godhead's heart. It is the heart that sees the
primordial eternity of every creature.*
—Hildegard of Bingen, 12th century Benedictine abbess,
Germany

GOD IS MADLY IN LOVE WITH US

*Of course, you had a beginning—that
moment in time when He created you
from nothing—yet your being has been
and shall always be in Him from
Eternity to Eternity, for He is
eternal.*
—Unknown author of *Cloud of Unknowing*

No one is quite sure who wrote the *Cloud of Unknowing*. He is known only as a 14th century Christian mystic. But whoever he was, he was madly in love with God and knew firsthand that God is madly in love with all of us. The author wrote the book to help people find a way to feel that love and that ecstasy that he felt when he communed with the Divine. That was in the 14th century. Times have changed. My guess is that not very many folks heard the cloud message back then. Today there are millions of books in print with the same basic message, and videos, and tapes, and speakers, and seminars. God is speaking to us in every bookstore and on radio and TV. Listen! We are never going to die. No being is going to die. God loves us too much to let us perish or vanish or lose our souls or our true natures. Each one of us and every rock and tree and animal and plant—all that is—is precious and tenderly treasured.

As we all contemplate this truth, it alters us at a deep level. Fear of death begins to move over and love of life both physical and eternal begins to take its place. Mourning our loved ones who have left their bodies behind can be softened by the knowledge that we are still united, though in a new way.

We are hearing stories of deceased grandparents, appearing as themselves, and rescuing or warning their grandchildren in an earthly crisis. We have only to go to the nearest bookstore to find a wealth of stories about angel visitations and near death experiences and miracles of all kinds. We are beginning to grasp just how much the Great Spirit adores us.

> *The lure of that heavenly place that I had*
> *glimpsed was very strong... the next 24 hours,*
> *while I was hovering between two dimensions of*
> *life, all the meanings of life and death seemed to*
> *pass before my inner eyes.*
> *Awareness came strong that the dying of the*
> *earthly body was not a calamity. Death was a*
> *natural transformation into*
> *another phase of living, where one could go right*
> *on joyfully progressing...The world we live in, and*
> *the world of my vision are really one.*

—Julia Phillips Ruopp, near death experience

> *... suddenly among them, I saw my father. I saw*
> *him as plainly as I ever saw him when he was*
> *alive...*
> *He smiled at me, and put up his hand in the old*
> *familiar gesture...Then he was gone, but in my*
> *heart the certainty of his presence was*
> *indisputable. He was there, and I know that some*
> *day, somewhere, I'll meet him again.*

—Norman Vincent Peale, 20th century minister

WE ARE CREATORS OF INFINITE LOVE

We are immortal, because we are made of love, and love is indestructible. When we 'make a friend', that is an act of creation. We literally create more love than was there before. When we feel a bond with someone, I believe we are feeling something that truly exists. Ordinarily we cannot see it with our physical eyes, yet we may sense it with our heart and solar plexus. I imagine if we could see it, it might look like a cord or ribbon of light connecting us with our beloved. This illumined line of love can stretch across the room or into another realm. And because this ribbon was woven by us in transcendent moments on God's enchanted loom, it can never fray, never unravel, never come undone.

Our loved ones are held fast to us and we to them. Though tears may fall from the eyes that cannot see our dear ones, though our hands may tremble at the loss of that familiar touch, yet our hearts in some deep place still feel the starlight flowing back and forth along the magic ribbon just as it always did.

I who am mortal and an insignificant person
in the world behold the entire creator of the
world in myself; and even while I live,
I embrace all blossoming life in myself
and know that I shall not die.

—Symeon, 10th century A.D. abbot, Constantinople

On the death of any living creature
this spirit returns to the spiritual
world, the body to the bodily world.

—Aziz Nasafi, 13th century Islamic mystic

OUR EXTRAORDINARY LOVEABLENESS

All of us are blessed with immortality. Not because we behave well or follow the rules of a certain religious doctrine. No. We are immortal, because we are immortal. We are made of God stuff. Our everlastingness has nothing to do with what we do. We don't earn it.

Perhaps, we could say, however, that what we do has something to do with our awareness of our everlastingness. As we begin to grasp the reality of our own immortality, very often our behavior begins to shift on its own. So that, instead of good behavior preceding everlasting life, the reverse seems to be more on the mark. It seems the more we become certain of our eternal nature, the more and more loving our behavior becomes.

Perhaps, it is because, the more fully conscious we become of our immortal nature, the more we can see our own radiant divinity; and, then, the more we fall in love with ourselves and all the other bright, luminous creatures sharing this earthly life with us.

Why? It's just that the logic begins to take hold. If God made us immortal, it must be because our Divine Creator wants us around or, to put it another way, God cannot bear to lose you or me. What can we conclude from this but that we must be fiercely loved? Therefore, there must be something extraordinarily lovable about us. And as we accept that fact, we find our old list of character 'flaws' and 'sins' blurring behind the bold blazing words from God—I LOVE YOU WITH AN ENDLESS LOVE. WE WILL ALWAYS BE TOGETHER YOU AND I—FOREVER AND EVER.

> *The soul never dies.*
> —Rabbi Menachen Mendel Schneerson,
> 20th century Jewish Rabbi

THE GRAND PARADOX: IMMORTALITY'S INTIMATE DANCE WITH DEATH

We witness the paradox of life and death each day. In the midst of eternal life, death abounds. At the same time, eternal life dwells passionately in the mortal cries of death. Out of the forest floor of dead and dying plants and animals ascend mammoth trees veined with rivers of life.

Yet, while death may be an illusion on a mystical level, here on the asphalt highway of earthly life, it visits us in very real ways. How can we accept our blessing of immortality when death seems to taunt us from every TV screen and newspaper and cemetery? In the Ripley's Believe It or Not museum in San Francisco, a gravestone is displayed inscribed with the words: "Here lies an atheist—all dressed up and no place to go." How tempting it is sometimes to think of life and death as opposites in the face of so much death and destruction.

We may be the first humans to have the technology to televise a war, live, on television sets around the world; to be told through every media, that species are becoming extinct and football fields of rain forest are disappearing while we drink our morning coffee. That children are starving to death in a war-torn African state and a plane just went down in the Atlantic, and people are drowning while we drive home from the office through heavy traffic. How can we sit blinking into this ever intensifying strobe light projection of violence and then reach out and receive our gift of eternal life? Let us see how it all comes together.

> *What rose and iris and carnation so intensely signified was nothing less than what they were—a transience that was yet eternal life, a perpetual perishing that was at the same time pure being...the Divine source of all existence.*
> —Aldous Huxley, 20th century English author, describing a personal psychedelic experience

EMBRACING THE PARADOX

While fierce winds of destruction threaten to erode away the vast mountain range of our eternality, we find that they are no match for the pure and steady upsurging of life demanding to live. I once observed a time-lapse film of a 'dead' mouse. The first few frames revealed a furry grey mouse lying on his side on the ground. Soon the tiny body became a moving mass of fly larvae. The shape-shifting continued until the end of the film when I beheld a tiny patch of translucent green stems rising from the brown earth. If we could leave that camera in that very spot for the next 10,000 years, such grand wonders would unfold as Life delighted in one form after another in an endless ring of manifestation.

Life and death are not polar opposites on a linear continuum, but rather, they are parts of each other in a timeless energy stream. Yet, deep in our communal memories, we hold the fear experienced by all the tribes that were ever destroyed by famine, disease, war, or disaster. Deep in our bones, we hold an inborn clawing instinct to keep the blood flowing in our veins. We spend enormous amounts of time and energy acquiring the stuff we need to keep our bodies and our families alive . And this stuff-getting is, all-in-all, very sacred work.

Yet, some say, we are deathless, eternal, spiritual beings. Aren't we supposed to rise above all this materialism? We can rise above it—yes—and at the same time, run our fingers through this sacred soil of life on earth. We are holy both in and out of our skin. Everything material is holy, and the ground, no matter where we stand or dig, is sacred ground.

Like comets trailing heaven's fire and light behind us, we have descended into matter. This does not mean that something heavenly has been contaminated or brought "down", nor that we have lost the Garden of Eden, for we carry the Garden with us wherever we go.

Rather, let us say that we are all seeds of God penetrating the Earth and being nourished by her. Our bodies and all matter are the result of the Big Holy Consummation. We are here in form, because Light is madly in love with Matter. Is it any wonder, then, that we light beings would be so profoundly attracted to material things and to keeping our bodies alive in form? This is deep, holy, creative work. This is the work of sending down roots and celebrating earth energy. Yet, at the same time, there is a part of us that keeps looking skyward, longing for the good old, nonlinear days when we were spirit energy, unhampered by the rootedness of physical hunger and material density, not to mention, pain.

Many monasteries have sought to provide lives of the least material so the monks and nuns would be free to contemplate the non-material behind closed eyes, to meditate upon "the cloud of unknowing" and the spring of living water. Paralleling that are all the kingdoms throughout history that have sought to provide lives of the most material, to claim the most territory and the most gold and the most power. We all live along this great experimental continuum, which, like life and death, travels in arcs and circles, not straight lines with beginnings and endings. We all hold within us the template hologram for the riches of kings and the wealth of renunciates. Let us embrace with our holy arms this vast diversity that we are—each one of us. For it is the matter-lover within us that has the capacity to see the sacred in the visible, and it is the heaven-lover within us that can dance to the music of heaven. Thus, we all are implicate cosmic ministers, finding infinite ways to marry heaven to earth.

The story of heaven falling in love with earth is told over and over. We are the bards of these tales, and we add our own embellishments as we go. And always the stories begin with the perception of polar opposites and end with the holy embrace of all.

In this first blessing, we find that we are immortal beings and that we never die. At the same time, our material bodies and possessions and loved ones' bodies must transform from time to time. So we mourn our losses, so many losses, and sometimes, in magic moments, we are able to simultaneously celebrate the transformations. The tiny mouse dies and baby grasses show up nourished by the flesh and decorated by the bones. Thus we see life and death in a wave form: life, death, life, death, life, coming in waves. They co-exist and co-create. They are the warp and woof of the rich tapestry of our adventures here. Death brings life brings death brings life.

Yet knowing this, we will still fight valiantly to prevent death and extinction and destruction and war. We cannot just be passive observers of this hypnotic wavy dance. There is some majestic dignity in fighting to live. A man who was falling to earth after his parachute failed to open seemed to be facing certain death, but thoughts of his loving family sparked a fire within him and perhaps rallied a number of angels to see to it that he survived. He imagined himself to be a bag full of laundry, and he landed just that way—limpand relaxed and alive.

In fighting for our health, for human rights, for animal rights, for peace, for old growth forests and wild rivers, for clean air, for rights of the yet-to-be born, for coming generations, we are acknowledging the sanctity of life in its present form. At the same time, it is the loss and death of an acre of rainforest that makes louder the outcry for its protection. And it is this symphonic sacred outrage that elevates all who truly hear it to a higher, more compassionate level of consciousness. Those who are deaf to the symphony, who cannot feel the sacredness of the ground that they slash and burn or who cannot sense the holiness of the children and animals they are killing, need as much compassion as the children and the trees, for they are disconnected from their own true nature. They do not know or recognize their own glory, but their knowing, like ours, will come, for we are in essence all one.

So we will fight on for life. The pain we feel at the physical loss of anyone precious to us is sometimes so intense that we can hardly bear it. Yet it is this very pain that shows us our extraordinary ability to love and our supreme courage in surrendering to a love that could break our hearts in an instant. How rich we become as a result of our yearnings and losses.

The painter is no less an artist because his exquisite painting has been burned in a fire. The mother and father are no less parents because their child has died of cancer. May I say—indeed their love and their parenthood have been fired and steeled as they walk the flaming coals of longing for the touch of their lost child's hand.

We are made of this longing for each other. God's energy is this longing—a round, embracing, fierce, and awesome hunger to be with us and to show us firsthand what love is. Times of loss are our best love-tutors. And with each loss, let us dive down into the depths of that love and, then, nearly drowning, find that we can breathe in that watery love as if it were air. Each time, coming up from those deep, dark pools, we have more wisdom and more compassion.

We are extraordinary creatures. We can simultaneously grieve and rejoice. Physical parting's pain says—Look! Look and see how vast and powerful and glorious is your love! When we feel that deep, fathomless love, that is God streaming through us.

It is a great mystery that we are eternal beings living on this planet with so many other eternal beings in skin and bark and feathers. With enough soil and microbes and tears, the sacred skin does indeed return to sacred dust. At the same time, paradoxically, we all live on to dance and play in some new way with the Creator of Joy who longs for us constantly.

> *Our minds are thus tuned or tunable*
> *to multiple dimensions, multiple*
> *realities...Our minds are time*
> *machines, able to sense the flow of*
> *possibility waves from both the*
> *past and the future.*
> —Fred Alan Wolf, 20th century American physicist

> *I believe in an immortal soul. Science*
> *has proved that nothing disintegrates*
> *into nothingness. Life and soul,*
> *therefore, cannot disintegrate into*
> *nothingness, and so are immortal.*
> —Werner von Braun, 20th century German scientist

THE CHAKRA CONNECTION:
FIRST BLESSING— IMMORTALITY
FIRST CHAKRA—SURVIVAL

The universe is very loving. It always seems to be finding ways to show us how everything is interconnected. There is much written and discussed these days about synchronicity. When we say a word and a split second later we hear the same word coming from our television set or see it on a billboard, that is synchronicity. When we think of a certain person and the next moment receive a call or letter from her or him, that is synchronicity.

When synchronicities happen, whether they are big events or small, we are getting in synch with the universe, glimpsing our internettedness. The Seven Blessings are no exception.

They fit quite neatly and synchronistically into many other sets of seven. Caroline Myss's recent book *Anatomy of the Spirit* is subtitled *The Seven Stages of Power and Healing*. These stages correspond to the seven chakras which she refers to as the "divine code". The stages and the chakras, she points out, also correspond to the seven Christian sacraments and the ten sefirot or tree of life of Judaism which, when certain ones are paired, can be counted as seven. All of these bear intriguingly close ties with our Seven Blessings.

The Seven Blessings correspond to the seven chakras so well that I decided to include in this book a description of each chakra along with its relationship to the blessing to which it belongs.

The chakra system is used in Eastern religions as well as among energy medicine practitioners, such as acupuncturists, reflexologists, and many others. The concept of chakras, or energy centers in the body, has been utilized for healing and spiritual practice for centuries. They are located in different areas of the body and are linked energetically with various glands, organs, and structural parts of the body. When the endocrine glands were isolated and named in the Western scientific community, they were found to exist right where the chakras had been seen intuitively by healers and mystics thousands of years earlier.

Endocrine glands secrete hormones into the blood stream. When glands are not functioning properly, we feel ill at ease or develop illnesses. When they are functioning at their peak, we may feel blissful and euphoric. Researchers have found high amounts of certain hormones in the blood of athletes, artists, yogis, and lovers when they are in states of euphoria.

Mystics and psychics, who can see the energy vortices created by the chakras in our bodies, see them as spinning wheels of color and light. In most chakra systems, the colors correspond to the seven colors of the rainbow. The first chakra at the base of the spine is usually seen as red; the second, located a few inches above the base of the spine, is usually orange, and so on to yellow, green, blue, indigo, and violet. Meditating with these colors can have a very healing effect.

CHAKRAS

7. Transcendence

6. Wisdom

5. Expression

4. Heart

3. Power

2. Relationships

1. Survival

BLESSINGS

7. Divinity

6. Perfection

5. Creativity

4. Love

3. Power

2. Belonging

1. Immortality

THE CHAKRA ~ BLESSING CONNECTION

It is possible also to tune into the seven musical notes in a scale that correspond to each chakra. In fact, you may find that you can discover the tone that fits each of your chakras. If you hum a very deep note you will notice that you feel it very low in your torso, right at the location of your root chakra at the base of your spine. As you try different notes going up the musical scale, while at the same time focusing on each chakra in turn, you will find the tone that feels right for each of your chakras. Just as meditating on chakra colors can be beneficial, humming a certain tone in meditation can be very healing for the part of the body to which that tone corresponds. More inter-connectedness. How awesomely organized and beautiful and musical is this universe of ours!

Many people are discovering that working directly with their chakras helps them heal and find wholeness, because it offers a way to focus on various parts of the sacred body and personality and gently integrate them and bring them together.

There are many methods of clearing and integrating the chakras. Acupuncture, reiki, herbal medicine, aromatherapy, foot reflexology, massage, visualization, meditation, and prayer all offer means of clearing and tuning these energy vortices. In addition to these healing modalities, I offer you this suggestion: As you contemplate each chakra in your meditation, take a moment to speak the blessing that corresponds to each chakra. Breathe the blessing into that area of your body. Meditating upon the chakras can have enormous physical and emotional benefits; the spiritual rewards can be even more astonishing. Carl von Weizsacher, director of the Max-Planck Institute for Life Sciences in Germany, sees the chakras as a pathway through which "nature seeks unity with God through man..." He declares that the person "who opens up that path for her is blessed by nature with the torrent of her bliss, with the realization of a new sphere of consciousness."

Now, may the blessing of this first chapter, that is the blessing of eternal life, comfort you at the place in you where your first chakra vibrates. The first chakra, sometimes called the basic chakra, is all about personal survival in a material world. It is energetically connected to the kidneys and spinal column. As infants, our bodies literally cannot survive unless someone feeds and protects us. So physical survival is the first order of business when we arrive here and take up residence in form. We instinctively know to cry out and alert our caretakers that we need to be fed and nurtured.

This first chakra is located at the base of the spine. It resonates with that area of the body, as well as the legs, feet, and the immune system. Close your eyes for a moment and focus your attention on that area of your body at the base of your spine. You may feel very primitive, survival type urges going on there. You may become more aware of your sense of being grounded, of being safe or not safe; you may sense strong desires, some sexual, some not, for things in the world that help us survive. This is the locus point, the boardroom, perhaps, from which you receive impulses to 'turn tail and run' or 'watch your tail'.

The first chakra holds many instinctive codes of behavior that help keep our bodies alive. Overly stressed, they can become blocked with fear and dread. Often physical symptoms will manifest in that area of the body, such as colitis, lower back pain, or immune-deficiency problems. These symptoms signal us that our first chakra needs attention. Instead of sending it loving attention, we may be communicating to it that we are afraid of dying, or afraid of deadly competition for a job or more customers, or that we're fearful of losing someone or something upon whom we believe our life depends.

The blessing of eternal life is asking us to let go of these fears, to understand that we, at the magnetic core of us, are ever living. Let us embrace the animal within us whose head jerks and turns, constantly searching the landscape for predators. Let us hold the infant within us that screams red-faced with the terror of helpless hunger. Let us soothe them both with the nourishment of the words: we are eternal; we live forever. It is within the jagged jaws of death that we see most clearly the brilliant light of our true nature. The ominous shadow of vultures' wings proves the very existence of light.

May we sit from time to time on the root of our soul as we pray, eyes closed, and know—there is harm, there is danger, and, at the same time, there is no harm and no danger. Let us send tendrils and rootlets down into the dark earth to hold us here and to hold the earth together like thick vines and long stemmed grasses do. Our souls know the sacred truth that our essence lives forever. Our bodies know the sacred task of resisting death and disintegration in order to keep these material elements and cells in this form we have chosen. And our hearts, being in the center of it all know this: it is in this grand holy tension between fighting death to the end and knowing there is no end—it is in that tension that ecstasy is born.

It is this ecstasy that many people who have clinically died and been revived have known. Though physically dead, they remained conscious of themselves as individual spirits who were totally loved and cared for in the heavenly realm they visited. After being revived, they were conscious of re-entering their physical bodies and relished a new sense of purpose, a new and compelling reason to keep the body alive in order to allow their spirit to do its earthly work.

So let us bless our first chakra. Let us imagine it relaxing, clearing, spinning peacefully, knowing it is an integral, sacred part of our journey as eternal beings learning who we are.

> *The water that I shall give will turn*
> *into a spring inside him, welling up*
> *to eternal life.*
> —Jesus Christ, John 4:14

EXPERIENCING THE BLESSING

Here is an exercise that may help you to experience the blessing of immortality that is yours. Write "I Am Eternal" at the top of a page. Now listen closely to the voices in your head that want to argue with that. Write them all down on a sheet of paper. Just write whatever comes to mind. It might look something like this:

"Who wants to live forever? Life is hard enough without going on and on."

"Who wants to sing in heaven for a billion years anyway?"

"My father just died. Life is very fragile. What difference does it make if life is eternal? He's still gone."

"Eternal life is irrelevant to me right now."

Now, listen to the voices within you that are saying "yes, I know this is true." What sort of dreamy images of an afterlife are they imagining?

When you feel you've finished, take a deep breath and gaze at your comments from the point of view of your higher, all-wise, eternal self. Feel your compassion for the earthly you that feels the pain and sadness and fear of death. Embrace the paradoxical and complex totality that is you. Invite into yourself your differences, your conflicts, your inconsistencies, and confusions—they are all of great significance, because they are part of you, and you are a great and holy being.

A PRAYER

*Oh, Blessed, Ever-nourishing
Father-Mother God*

*You—who have given us the moon
    and the stars,
You—who course through us like
    a mighty river,
You—whom we name, though you are
    unnamable,
Help us to understand and accept that
    we are everliving spirits.
Help us to somehow grasp that we are
    Pure Love and You are Love. All
    one seamless garment of passionate
    adoration are we with You.
Help us to comprehend that all our tears
    and losses and deaths are counted,
    each one precious, each one a mother
    of new life.
Thank you, beautiful Lord, for hearing
this prayer, for holding our hands as we
say it, and for assuring us that it is
answered even as the words flow from our lips.
                    Om Amen Ho*

2nd

BLESSING

YOU BELONG

Without you, I would not be complete, nor would Life, nor Love. You are part of the One Divine Cosmic Family. Absolutely everyone and everything is connected in this great sea of Love. Without you, We are not whole. You are wanted and adored.

The Blessing of Belonging

How we need this blessing! In this world where we so often have felt separate and alone, the truth is shining more and more brightly through the clouds of our fears: We are All One.

Namaste [a greeting which means]:
I honor the place in you in which the
entire universe dwells. I honor the
place in you which is of love, of truth,
of light, and of peace. When you are
in that place in you, and I am in that
place in me, we are one.
—Hindu greeting

Mitakuye Oyas'in [Native American
Lakota words which mean]:
All My Relations! [spoken in
ceremonies to honor the fact that we
are all related to each other and to
the stones and animals and plants.
We are all part of the Holy family.]
—Lakota blessing

Hold a single strand of your hair up to the sunlight and very close to your eyes. Hold it so that you can see the refraction of the sunlight on your hair. You will see all the colors of the rainbow glinting like tiny jewels along a multitude of parallel microfilaments that appear to be strands of pure light. That is only one hair on your head—just one.

If you have a faceted diamond or gem of some kind, hold it up to the corner of your eye, perhaps less than an inch away. Catch the light of the sun and survey once again the glorious colors and light. You and the diamond and I—we are all multihued, brilliant fountains of light.

What if we could look from a distance at a scene of forest, creek, birds, wildlife, children, stones, earth, and grass; what if we could see the rainbows all at once in the fur and hair and feathers and scales; in the bubbling creek water, waving grass, and sparkling stones? Could we bear the burning brilliance of this vista bathed in crayon colors and illuminated like stars? Could we mark the points at which a child's outstretched hand ends and the tip of a bluebird's wing begins?

Some people can see at least some of this radiance in the form of auras and energy streams and fields. Kirlian photography has recorded a bit of it on film. We walk, work, play, sleep, and make love in a cosmic sea of color and light. It is no accident that we are here. This cosmic sea is our home. Each one of us and every seed and egg and stone is a completion, a deep satisfaction, a soothing lullaby to every other being. *We* cannot be without *you*.

My husband and I boarded a plane for California one winter morning just before sunrise. We flew below the clouds in the grey pre-dawn sky while we gained altitude. Suddenly, our plane broke through the heavy clouds. We gazed out our window at the new brightness and saw, to our astonishment, a rainbow, but this was no ordinary rainbow. What we saw was a complete and perfect circle of vivid hues. All the colors were there, but instead of the usual arc, the entire circle appeared. Where was the treasure at the end of the rainbow if there was no end? Now we know—the prize is the endless bow itself, this perfect, unbroken circle of prismatic life—of which you and I are an essential, needed part.

And it seems to help to have a rather high angle of view to see the wholeness that we are and to see that the mythical treasure at the end of the rainbow is, in fact, not at the end, but dwells within its endless connectedness.

> *God is a circle whose center is every-*
> *where and its circumference nowhere.*
> —Empedocles, 6th century, B.C., Greek philosopher

YOU ARE A RIVER OF LIGHT

Imagine, for a moment, yourself to be a riverbed cradling a fast moving stream. Your head is at the headwaters, and your toes point out to sea. Feel your water run and swell and move stones and trickle and fall and mist as you cradle it within your rooted banks. Observe how the deer drink from your waters and the trout swim within you. See the osprey searching your depths from a tree branch above. Feel the turtle squishing his little feet into the mud at the edge of your water, and hear the dragonflies whirring. Feel the tendrils of willow roots as they slowly penetrate through your banks seeking water and helping you hold the soil together.

This sweet imagining is not so far from who you really are, for the divine and very liquid river of light and life does indeed flow through you in an endless moving stream.

> *Many modern discoveries help man*
> *to apprehend the cosmos as a varied*
> *expression of one power—light,*
> *guided by divine intelligence.*
> —Paramahansa Yogananda, Hindu yogi, teacher

YOUR BIG HOLY FAMILY

> *The world and I have a common*
> *origin and all creatures and I*
> *together are one.*
> —Chuang Tzu, 3rd century, B.C., Taoist, China

A drop of rain falls to earth in late June and, by October, finds its way to your lips and moistens your tongue and penetrates your cells. Then you, in your infinite biological wisdom, breathe the raindrop out in vapor and share it with a nearby leaf. The droplet carries with it now the collective vibrations of the pouring rain, the racing rivers, you, and now the leaf. How many drops of water have passed intimately through you and carried your precious name up into the clouds?

While the fish swim and the birds soar for us, we walk the soft earth for them. We are blessed with infinite connectedness. Like Jesus' seamless robe, we all fit together with such perfection that we can never be torn apart or divided into pieces. Just as a family is related and bonded by blood, genes, and history, so our Big Family and all our relations are intimately interconnected by holy vibrations and cosmic history.

> *Life in me cannot be other than*
> *the life in a blade of grass...The same*
> *underground river nourishes all life,*
> *all existence.*
> —Howard Thurman, 20th century minister

IF YOU'RE HERE, THERE'S A REASON

If you woke up this morning—if you can breathe on a mirror and leave a little mist, then God still needs you to be here, and we all need you as well.

We are all here in these physical bodies on earth in this space time continuum for one thing—Love. We are here to learn how to love, to learn how to be loved, to learn how to love ourselves, indeed, to learn that we are love. Everything we do revolves around love. If we still have love to learn, receive, and give, in ways that can only happen in our present bodies, then we will continue to be in our bodies. When we are finished learning what we can here, then we go on to the next realm to learn about love in new ways.

I knew a man so bereft of hope that he thrust the barrel of a gun into his mouth and pulled the trigger. He was utterly convinced that he had no purpose in being here. Imagine his shock when he awoke in the hospital, still living and breathing. It simply wasn't time for him to leave his body and go to the next realm. He was not through with his work and his lessons that only earth can provide. He was needed here.

Most people who have had near death experiences, though they hunger for the peace and bliss of the afterlife that embraced them, at the same time seem to have a renewed zest for life on planet earth. They have a feeling that they are here for a reason; that they have a mission; that Great Spirit has a plan for their lives.

Perhaps, you have never had a close call with death. Nevertheless, think over all the ways your body could have ended its days in just the past week—a car accident, a fall? Yet you are here reading this book. That is a miracle. Your sacred heart still beats. Why? Simply this: you still have things to learn about love on earth, and you still have love to share, that only you, absolutely only you, in all your uniqueness, can give. You are living out a divine plan. You really are on a mission from God.

> *What we do is less than a drop in the*
> *ocean. But if that drop were missing,*
> *the ocean would lack something.*
> —Mother Teresa, 20th century Catholic nun

> *Distinctions of "important" and*
> *"unimportant" are surely unknown to*
> *the Lord, lest, for want of a pin, the*
> *cosmos collapse!*
> —Paramahansa Yogananda, 20th century Hindu

THE ECSTASY OF ONENESS

> *The day of my spiritual awakening*
> *was the day I saw and knew I saw*
> *all things in God and God in all things.*
> —Mechtild of Magdeburg, 13th century social activist

> *I saw more than I can tell and I*
> *understood more than I saw; for*
> *I was seeing in a sacred manner the*
> *shapes of all things in the spirit, and*
> *the shape of all shapes as they must*
> *live together as one being.*
> —Black Elk, 19th and 20th century Native American
> Oglala Sioux shaman

When people describe their own ecstatic unions with God, they nearly always describe such a union as an experience of oneness with everything and everyone. It doesn't seem to matter where or when they lived or what religion, if any, they practiced. It is what Matthew Fox, director of the Institute of Creation Spirituality, calls the "holy omnipresence of the Divine One in all things," also known as "panentheism." This ecstatic union experience awakens us to the blessing of oneness, awakens us to the remembrance that we cannot possibly be alone, no matter how lonely we may feel. We are, as mystics and shamans have declared for centuries, one with the universe.

Our skin artfully covers the sculptural lines of our bodies. We can measure the size and weight of our physical covering, but our spirit ranges far beyond such temporal borders and interlaces with All-That-Is. It is we—as pure spirits—that know we are all one and long to bring that awareness into our brains and cells and personalities; it is we, *spirits of ecstasy that we are*, that can hold a slice of orange up to the sun and say: "Behold, the entire juicy universe is before us, translucent and succulent!" And we are dearest kin to such a miracle as that.

> *The Kingdom of God is not coming*
> *with signs to be observed; nor will*
> *they say, 'Look, here it is!' or 'There*
> *it is!' for behold, the kingdom of God*
> *is in your midst.*
> —Jesus Christ, Luke 17:20-21

YOU ARE LIMITLESS LIGHT AND ENERGY

Just as Sarah's surgery was nearly finished, her heart stopped beating. During the less than 60 second period before she was revived, she "saw" the operating room and hallway in great detail. When she awoke, she recalled the names on the surgery schedule tacked up in the hall, the color of the sheets, the anesthesiologist's unmatched socks, a nurse's hairstyle. She also accurately recalled the conversation between nurses and doctors during the crisis. This would be amazing enough for a sighted person, but Sarah was born blind.

What does this mean? It means that Sarah's mind is not con-fined to her body and her physical senses. Nor is *your* mind con-fined to your body or your physical senses. Your mind, your soul, your self are all nonlocal. To physicists, nonlocality refers to the concept that, at the subquantum level, location ceases to exist. According to David Bohm's interpretation of quantum physics, all points in space are equal to each other. He concludes that nothing is separate from anything. Everything is interconnected.

What we are discovering (or, shall we say, remembering) is that we ourselves are nonlocal. We, *beings of light and energy that we are*, are not limited by our five senses, nor by our epidermis, nor by the walls of our homes or the roads we travel. We are not, in our essence, isolated and disconnected. We are, rather, inter-connected with all that lives and thinks and loves and contains the being of God, and that is everything, absolutely everything.

> *Deep down the consciousness of mankind is one.*
> —David Bohm, 20th century physicist

> *In this emptiness the two are indis-tinguishable and each contains in itself the whole world.*
> —Sengstan, Third Zen Ancestor

> *...Each object in the world is not merely itself, but involves every other object and, in fact, is every-thing else.*
> —Avatamsaka Sutra, ancient Sanskrit text

NO PATH NEEDEST THOU

> *Path presupposes distance; if He be near, no path needest thou at all. Verily it maketh me smile to hear of a fish in water athirst!*
> —Kabir, 15th century, mystic and poet from India

We look down the road at our departing friend, and, with our eyes, we see distance, empty space, and separation. Physicists and mystics tell us to *look a little more closely*. That seemingly empty space contains more energy than the energy that exists in the matter in our own bodies. If all the energy were somehow removed from our bodies, the dense matter remaining might not even be visible to the naked eye. It is energy that connects us. Like the lacy green branches of a forest of trees, we also are laced and tatted together with All Energy in intricate, infinite, intimate patterns.

Some physicists are now saying that the quantum wave function is an aspect of God. It is a term being used to talk about what holds all the atoms together. It is a wave of mind stuff, a wavy weaver of the undulating universe. It is the stuff that makes things visible and exists among all that is visible, holds it together and loves it.

> *Know that with one single fraction*
> *of my being I pervade and support*
> *the universe, and know that I am.*
> —Bhagavad Gita 10:42

YOU ARE LOVE SET FREE

> *Every visible and invisible creature*
> *is a theophany or appearance of God.*
> —John Erigena, 9th century Irish philosopher

> *I see something of God each hour of*
> *the twenty-four,*
> *And each moment then,*
> *In the faces of men and women*
> *I see God,*
> *And in my own face in the glass.*
> *I find letters from God dropt in*
> *the street,*

And everyone is sign'd by God's name
And I leave them where they are,
For I know that wheresoe'er I go,
Others will punctually come
For ever and ever.

—Walt Whitman, 19th century American poet

Your consciousness, your soul, your eternal self dwells in subtle realms beyond space and time. These are realms of vibration and light where all is whole, interconnected, and replete with order. You carry within and around you the foundational strength of solid stones; the sensuous nourishment of warm summer rain; the fearsome, transformative power of the blazing sun; and the enlivening lightness of air. You carry within you *the very breath of God.*

On the material plane, we display our interwoven nature with the warp and woof of telephone wires, electric cable, gas, water, and sewer lines. Highways, rivers, flyways, time lines, radar, microwaves, satellite telemetry, and now the Internet. We cannot seem to resist finding more and more explicate ways to outpicture our implicate oneness, this profound and original, native internettedness. All those pathways have always been there among us, but we couldn't see them. So we made them visible and filled our skies with wires and our earth with roads.

Australian aborigines, who still survive in wilderness areas, communicate quite well over long distances using mental telepathy, according to some observers. They are also apparently able to communicate with the earth and find water and food without maps, instruments, or tools other than the sticks and stones which happen to be handy. Somehow these folks remembered that they could communicate with each other and with the universe because they were one with all. The memory is within us as well. Have you ever had a thought of someone and then, right after the thought, seen them or had a phone call from them? Can this vestigial knowing of ours be reawakened and put to use? Why not?

This physical universe is a metaphor, that is, a symbolic representation of Divine Reality. When we see phone lines and microwave towers, these are crude (even damaging) representations of the fact that we are divinely connected to each other with invisible filaments of light and vibrations. Each one of us is a metaphor as well, a hologram of Heaven, a representation of the Divine. *You are love set free to see love everywhere, as in a mirror reflected back to you.*

> *To become divine is to become*
> *attuned to the whole of creation.*
> —Mahatma Gandhi, 20th century Indian
> spiritual leader

> *One thing I learned was that we are*
> *all part of one, big, living universe.*
> *If we think we can hurt another*
> *living thing without hurting our-*
> *selves, we are sadly mistaken. I look*
> *at a forest or a flower or a bird now,*
> *and say 'that is me, part of me.' We*
> *are connected with all things, and if*
> *we send love along these connections,*
> *then we are happy.*
> —Near death experiencer, 20th century

THE GRAND PARADOX: THE INTIMATE DANCE OF ONENESS WITH SEPARATION

While in some fine moments, we sense our deep connection to all life and feel God abiding in our cells and smiles; yet there are times for us all when we gaze at the outline of our unheld hands and cry, "I am alone."

We are all divine-love-energy diving into separate forms in order to see, hear, taste, and smell how beautiful we are. The irony is that after slipping into these separate molds, we see edges of ourselves we never saw before. We feel cut off from each other. We forget.

We took on these forms so we could gasp with audible voices at the visions of grace before our new eyes. We wanted to *in-form* ourselves about our common radiance from a different viewpoint in the space-time continuum. However, once we incarnated into these bodies many of us forgot our divine origins, forgot that we were spiritual beings seeking physical experiences. We forgot that we are transformers of love, and that we and God-within-us are seeking ever new ways to birth love into matter.

It's not much comfort to talk about our connectedness to each other when our husband has just left for another woman or our best friend has died? When you see your friendly neighbor every day and suddenly she is transferred across the country, that feels very much like separation. Likewise, it's very difficult to feel connected and loving to those who speak out against us or physically attack us or take our money? We don't want to be connected to them. We want distance from them. In fact, much is being written now about setting personal boundaries, protecting ourselves from others who would take advantage of us or treat us disrespectfully. In addition to that, there is much to be said about celebrating our uniqueness, and honoring the things that make us separate and different and special. All of that seems to contradict the idea that we are all interconnected.

It is in non-ordinary states of consciousness, altered mystical moments of awareness that we are privy to our true state of oneness. By contrast, it is in our waking, everyday, survival mode that we comprehend fully our need to protect ourselves and our families and friends. It is good not to listen to a meditation tape while driving, for example. In order to drive a car safely, we have to believe in separation, so our car doesn't become one with another car.

I remember Annie, a young woman who was eventually diagnosed with bipolar disorder. It started, as most, if not all, "mental illnesses" do, with a spiritual emergency. Her spirit was emerging and crying out for recognition. Unfortunately, Annie was ill-prepared and did not know what was happening to her. First she saw Jesus clearly visible in the sky. Then, she heard a voice directing her to drive to Minneapolis from her home in Kansas City. She got in her car in an extremely altered state of ecstasy and drove over 100 miles per hour until the highway patrolmen were finally able to convince her to stop. In her ecstatic state of mind, she felt her oneness, her invulnerability, but in her inexperience with such states, she risked serious injury to herself and her fellow travelers.

We all understand the label "do not operate heavy machinery when taking this medication." In a sense, our bodies are heavy, dense machinery. When we first gain access to heaven's bliss through prayer or meditation, most of us can only function on that level if the body is sitting or otherwise not occupied with earthly activities. Saint Teresa of Avila had many practical and organizational responsibilities and was even heard to complain, at times, that her ecstasies came so often she could not get all her work done. Her life and work and that of many other mystics show us that we need not deny our sense of oneness and connection in order to survive physically. We can experience both if we *practice remembering who we are.*

It is when we forget our unitive origins that we tense up with loneliness and fear. It is this loneliness and fear which moves us to claim allegiance to a small tribe or species or age group and see all other beings as competitors for food, territory, money, and health, even life itself.

It is the earth-based sensation of separateness and its companion, fear, that has led human beings to enslave, torture, kill and experiment on billions of people and animals and plants that were seen as separate and different from those in power. Power over others is the grand illusory antidote to fear. Our own spirits tell us that the true antidote to fear is love and compassion. That love and compassion grows and develops as we begin to see behind the paradox. Because we are, in truth, *all one*, when we care for ourselves lovingly, we are automatically caring for others. When we care lovingly for others, we are automatically caring for ourselves.

*Unless the self expands to cover the
entire creation of God, there can be
no permanent peace.*
—Kirpal Singh

*Until he extends the circle of his
compassion to all living things, man
will not himself find peace.*
—Albert Schweitzer, 20th century physician

So how do we do that? How do we extend the circle of our compassion and still take care of ourselves?

EMBRACING THE PARADOX

The challenge of this great paradox, of course, is once again to learn the elegant embrace. Let us allow ourselves to feel and face the fears that our aloneness brings and the fears that arise when our boundaries are invaded, and let us hold those fears near to us. They are an essential part of us at this time in our evolution. They are very precious. Sometimes they warn us of impending danger; sometimes they challenge us to search our hearts for more courage. They are to be honored simply because they are part of us, and we are worthy to be honored; and they are to be honored because they come bearing gifts of wisdom if we can hold them long enough.

Now while we hold this pain and fear within us; may we also, at the same time, acknowledge as best we can, our oneness with All Creation. Holding and acknowledging and honoring two opposites has a curious effect if one holds them long enough. Instead of remaining in the cognitive dissonance of two apparently opposing views, we begin to switch into bi-level awareness where our *all-oneness* becomes an integral part of our *al-oneness*. Can we allow the possibility that we are both lonely and surrounded by love, both private and open, both defended from all and protected by all?

How delicious to feel both the fearsome lonely power of

the self-aware-of-itself and the surrender to the safety of the Cosmic womb! The God and Goddess-in-us is constantly seeking rhythmic separation—union—separation—union—separation—union. For unity is so sweet when seen from a distance. It is all the same dance. Some of the steps move away from the Divine Partner so we can shimmy and shake. Some steps move us back into the arms of our Beloved where we merge together in blissful embrace.

Let us honor our loneliness and celebrate the compassion that can bring, and let us have faith in our oneness and celebrate the love that it can bring. It's all for love. Everything comes to us for love. Everything teaches us love. You cannot be abandoned, but you can *feel* abandoned. And while your tears of loneliness fall to the earth, God is planting seeds at your feet.

> *It is in union with the other that I*
> *find my true self. Incredible para-*
> *dox?...In the deepest and most loving*
> *union with another, far from losing*
> *ourselves, we discover our deepest*
> *selves at the core of our being. If this*
> *is true of human relationships, it*
> *must also apply to the most intimate*
> *union of all: that of Yahweh with*
> *His people.*
> —Unknown author of *Cloud of Unknowing*, 14th century Christian mystic

THE CHAKRA CONNECTION: SECOND BLESSING—BELONGING SECOND CHAKRA—RELATIONSHIPS

May the blessing of unity and belonging comfort you at the place in you where your second chakra vibrates.

The second chakra, sometimes called the sacral chakra, is concerned with relationships. It is located in the lower abdominal area. It corresponds physically and vibrationally to the sexual organs and to the lower back. This chakra is all about connecting up with others and finding partners as part of our survival in the space-time-earth realm. It contains many codes, some as simple as seductive hip movements to attract the opposite sex. Some are much more complex. All are designed to help us find ways to belong, to be part of a group, to feel safe and loved.

When we feel abandoned, betrayed, and cut off, fear often becomes the knife in the ribs that shoves us into reconnecting. Sometimes we reconnect in ways that hurt. Shirley, a gifted and loving social worker had left behind her a childhood full of abandonment and abuse. Desperate to belong with someone, she proceeded into a future marked by four marriages. She unconsciously attracted men who abused and abandoned her each time. Her need to be loved and belong was tangled up with her need for her abusive parents to love her. So she was attracted to men with traits similar to her mother and father. She was unconsciously drawn to men who would replay her childhood traumas with her. The unconscious need is to keep reliving the drama until we get it right, until it is resolved and healed.

Eventually, this brilliant woman, who had helped so many of her clients create better lives for themselves, could no longer deny the obvious pattern. Courageously she extricated herself from the last relationship and remained single for many years. It was during that time without a partner that she turned within herself for a sense of belonging and self-acceptance. Eventually, with the wisdom in her heart that she deserved to be treated with dignity and mature love, she found her soul mate.

In addition to behavior patterns such as Shirley's, this chakra area may also be involved in sending physical warning signals from the various organs in the area telling us that we have blocked our emotions at this level of our psyche. If we receive such a signal from that area of our body, we are being asked to literally look within and listen to the body. Thus, we will hear, through the parable of the body itself, what our next step in spiritual growth is. For example, if you develop a physical ailment in your uterus or testicles, what might be the message? Both of these organs are symbolic of bringing forth new life, of creativity, of nurturing, of pure feminine or masculine energy. Perhaps, your body is telling you that you need to attend to your own passion for creating a work of art. Or, perhaps, it is signaling you that you are not valuing your femaleness or your maleness, and so, by not receiving the honoring it needs, this organ has become weak.

In these ways, chakras help you receive a clear idea of the next step to take on your path of learning to honor yourself as a divine being. Thus, you can begin to show that part of your body, and its symbolic counterpart in your soul, the reverence and care and prayer it needs. Of course, in addition to becoming conscious of these needs, you may also require therapeutic intervention such as medical assistance, herbs, dietary changes, etc., and these are all forms of honoring as well.

Let us bless our second chakra. Let us feel it spinning peacefully, humming, vibrating in synchrony with divine rhythm. The Universe is chanting Ommm, and Amennn, and Onnnne, we are Onnnnne.

> *Everything that is active, that moves*
> *or breathes, every physical, astral, or*
> *animate energy, every fragment of*
> *force, every spark of life, is equally*
> *sacred; for in the humblest atom and*
> *the most brilliant star, in the lowest*
> *insect and the finest intelligence,*
> *there is the radiant smile and thrill*
> *of the same absolute.*
> —Pierre Teilhard de Chardin, 20th century theologian

EXPERIENCING THE BLESSING OF ONENESS

1. You can do this exercise with a small group of people. Have a volunteer leave the room, so that person will not hear the group plan. Instruct the remaining participants to think a series of thoughts that are first positive, then negative, then

negative again, then positive thoughts. Tell them you will nod
each time they are to change to a different set of thoughts.
Bring the volunteer back and have her stand in front of you.
You must be visible to the group so the members can see you
nod. Now instruct the volunteer to think only positive, uplifting thoughts. Have her extend an arm out perpendicular to her
body. Using a method known as kinesiology, apply downward
pressure on her arm, while she tries to hold it in place. You will
apply this downward pressure right after each nod. You should
notice that the volunteer is less able to resist the downward
pressure when the group has been signaled to think negative
thoughts. This demonstrates how we are connected to each
other in body, mind, and soul; and it demonstrates the power
of our very thoughts to affect each others' physical and emotional strength.

2. Find a tree whose branches you can reach. Hold one
branch in each hand. Imagine Divine energy pouring into the
top of the tree and into the top of your head. Feel the light vibrate through your body and out through your left arm into
the tree branch you are holding and then coursing through the
tree, spreading out through all the branches and making its way
to the other branch you are holding with your right hand. Allow the energy to swirl and undulate around and through you
and the tree, you and the tree, with more Divine energy constantly pouring through you both. Feel your connection to
each other as you dance together in the cosmic energy stream.

A PRAYER

Oh, Beautiful Lord,

Everything You touch is sacred,
And You have touched everything.

And, thus, You have made us holy and part of Your sacred cosmic family. Thank You for our brothers and sisters—the birds, the wolves, the deer, the fish, the rocks, the trees, the yet-to-be-born, the manifest and the unmanifest, the energy and the matter, our beautiful blue-green, ever-nurturing Earth Mother, the planets and stars—All in whom You dwell and through whom You bless us all.

Help us to understand that when we feel separate, abandoned and alone, that You are in our sadness and our longing; that, in fact, You dwell within each one of our tears; and that You will find a way to comfort us and hold us in Your arms.

You are in each flower that fills our senses with delight,
You are in each bird that sends our hearts soaring in flight,
You are in each gentle hand that has ever caressed us tenderly,
And in every lover's kiss.
Thank You, oh Creator of Holy Omnipresence within and around us all, for Your unifying, comforting, undying Love.

Om Amen Ho

3rd

BLESSING

YOU ARE POWERFUL

I am the Power of Love. Your cells and your breathing; your thoughts and your longings all vibrate with that Power. You breathe in my awe-some Love for you and all creation. You breathe out your electrifying Love for All-That-Is. You are Heaven brought to Earth.

The Blessing of Power

Jesus told us we could do greater things even than he. Masters and saints, yogis and shamans from every place and time agree.

> *Though we are God's sons and daughters,*
> *we do not realize it yet.*
> —Meister Eckhart, 13th and 14th century German
> theologian and mystic

> *Is it not written in your law, 'I said,*
> *"You are Gods" '?*
> —Jesus Christ, John 10:34

Where is the power in a lightning bolt? Is it in the fiery fingers that we see, or is it in the electric energy that we don't see? Seen or unseen, the power is there. But the bright white bolt lets us know it's there; let's us see God's big, bold, pyrotechnic power.

We are like lightning flashing. We make God's power visible. Just look at you. The fact that there is a you. *What an astonishing miracle*! Every little movement you make, every word you speak are all miracles, every crescent moon on your fingernails, every line on your hands. *What extraordinary beauty*! And your smile—surely your smile alone carries the voltage of a thousand lightning bolts. Divine power moves through us like a river, ever ready to connect, to create, to love, to move.

Corrie Ten Boom, a Dutch woman imprisoned in a Nazi concentration camp for hiding Jewish people, knew what it felt like to be flooded by the power of God's love. Corrie may well have been one of the most compassionate people on earth, but one evening after giving a speech on forgiveness, her compassion was challenged beyond her own personal strength. There, coming toward her out of the audience, was a former Nazi. Corrie immediately recognized him to be the one who had been primarily responsible for her sister's death in the prison camp where they were both held so many years ago.

Apparently responding quite emotionally to her speech, the man, upon reaching her, held out his hand to Corrie and asked her to forgive him for what he had done. Speechless, Corrie hesitated, thinking only God can do this, for she knew she could not do it alone. She asked God to take over. Immediately, her arm lifted without her volition, and her hand took hold of the German man's hand. As she touched his hand, a powerful heat and electricity rushed through her. She was suddenly filled with a compassion that she knew was not her own. Thus, she came to know firsthand the onrushing love God has for each one of us, no matter who we are or what we have done.

This very same power is constantly moving through each one of us. As we awaken to that inner knowing, we draw closer to activating it. Fire burns, invisible in the unmanifested realm, until we take the initiative to strike a match and light a candle.

YOU ARE A CHILD OF LIGHT

> *Einstein repeats the idea of Christ ('I am the light')...when he tells us that light is at the boundary between matter and vibration (spirit).*
> —Irving Oyle, 20th century American physician

> *If therefore thine eye be single, thy whole body shall be full of light.*
> —Jesus Christ, Matthew 6:22

> *I know I was sitting in the middle of darkness, but while I was there surrounded by darkness, you appeared as light. You lit me up completely by your light. I became light in the night.*
> —Symeon, 10th century abbot

You are filled with power, because you are filled with God. You are literally made of the power of the Divine Creator. Recall some times in your life when you felt powerless. Always, those are times when we forget who we are. It is impossible for the Big Holy's beloved children to have power failures, because our power station is not nuclear, not hydro, not coal fired. Our source of inner fire and electricity can't melt down or burn up or collapse in a flood. If a light bulb were made of light, it would never go out. We are made of light. We are the children of the "Father of Lights". What wonders can we do?

THE AWESOME POSSIBILITIES

Almighty powers are shut in nature's cells.
—Sri Aurobindo, 20th century Indian yogi

Newtonian physics supports the "strong objectivity principle". This is the belief that matter acts on its own unaffected by the observer. Quantum physicists have discovered, however, that activity at the quantum level is directly affected by the scientist observing it. In other words, the state of mind of the observer and the intention of that observer directly affect activity on the quantum level. Our minds and intentions directly influence the movement of electrons which are considered to be the smallest units of matter. This "observer effect" means any one of us can and do have an impact on tiny bits of matter simply with our thoughts. How can this be?

It is because we are not local beings. Our minds are not confined to our bodies. Electrons are nonlocal as well. This means that our consciousness and electrons both exist somehow beyond space and linear time. Not confined or limited by the factors of space and time, we, as spiritual beings, have power over space and time.

Spirit *your spirit, my spirit, Great Spirit* is weak-kneed in love. This love, like the observing physicist's intention, spins and caresses electrons until they form patterns, visible patterns which become what we think of as physical bodies. As a result, we spirits can visibly see the object of our desire and love it all the more. These bodies are made of God's and our desire to love. They are made of the nonlocal, intensely focused power of love. Do you see how powerful you are?

If you see weakness when you look at yourself in the mirror, you are forgetting that the body you see before you is proof of the power of your love. Indeed, it would not be the pulsating, rotating dance of electrons that it is without the powerful love of your spirit intending, willing, and seducing it into manifestation.

Jesus showed us what we spirits are capable of doing with our bodies. He calmed the seas, turned water into wine, brought the dead back to life, and found money in the mouth of a fish. Paramahansa Yogananda reported that the body of St. John of the Cross who died in 1591, was exhumed in 1859. The body showed no signs of decomposition much to the shock and wonder of those present at the exhumation. Yogananda explained that great saints understand that the body and all matter is condensed energy and that energy is manipulatable.

In his autobiography, Yogananda mentions many saints and yogis who live without eating: Giri Bala of India, Therese Neumann, St. Lidwina of Schiedam, Blessed Elizabeth of Rent, St. Catherine of Siena, Dominica Lazarri, St. Nicholas of Flue and many others. The Christian saints he listed were also stigmatists, meaning that, periodically, bleeding wounds appeared on their bodies exactly where Jesus was wounded at the crucifixion.

Therese Neumann, a German Catholic mystic and stigmatist, born in 1898, became blind and paralyzed in an accident at the age of 20. Five years later she was miraculously healed through prayer. Thereafter, she neither drank nor ate anything except one little consecrated wafer each day. In 1926, she began bleeding at weekly intervals from her hands, feet, head, and chest, exactly as Jesus had done on the cross so many centuries before.

When asked how she lives without food, Therese told

Yogananda, "I live by God's light." "How Einsteinian," wrote Yogananda as he pondered her response in his memoirs. In spite of her weekly bleeding and lack of food, Therese seemed always full of energy and vitality. Many people visited her over the years and received healings by being in her presence.

Trailanga Swami, a yogi from India, was reputed to have drunk poisons with no effect, to have sat on top of the water floating on the Ganges for days, and to have floated under the waves without coming up for air. When he was repeatedly jailed for walking around in public in the nude, he simply disappeared from his jail cell until finally the police gave up trying to incarcerate him and did their best to ignore his nudity.

These are supreme examples of human beings fine tuning energy with matter and aligning their will with the will of Awesome Love. What about us, though: we householders, homemakers, parents, business people, artists, athletes, children and students, indeed all of us? Even if we never walk on water or through walls, we will nevertheless perform miracles in our lifetimes. Look around. There is evidence everywhere of our overarching powers to bring love into being.

The Kearneys were sharecroppers with 17 children. Undaunted by the appearance of their situation, they believed that every one of their children would escape the poverty the Kearneys had always known. Through faith, prayers, and dogged determination, 15 of the children have graduated from college, and the other two may yet finish as well. There are literally uncountable stories like the Kearneys' of the power of the human spirit overcoming seemingly impossible odds.

> *By unlocking at all risks his human doors, [man] is caught up into the life of the universe, his speech is thunder, his thought is law...*
> —Ralph Waldo Emerson, 19th century poet

> *All things are possible to him that believeth.*
> —Jesus Christ, Mark 9:23

THE UNIVERSE WANTS TO GIVE YOU THE DESIRES OF YOUR HEART

The winds of grace blow all the time.
All we need to do is set our sails.
—Sri Ramakrishna Paramahansa, 19th century Indian mystic

One evening, just at dusk, gravel crunched under my tires as I pulled out of the wilderness area parking lot. Though my attention was focused on the road ahead, 'something' caused me to turn my head to the left. I could just barely make out a small form half buried in the gravel. Curious, I stopped and retrieved a dusty knife. With no name on it and looking as though it had been lost a good while, I felt the universe was asking me to pass it on.

Almost at that same moment, back at home, my husband was flipping through an outdoor equipment catalog. Coming to the page of pocket knives, he wishfully circled the one he wanted. When I arrived home with the resurrected knife, he rushed to show me the knife he had circled. It was exactly the same.

This, of course, was beyond coincidence. It is what we now call synchronicity. Now this knife was something my husband could have ordered himself. It was not that expensive. Why would the universe go to so much trouble to help him manifest that knife? I believe that it was not the knife so much that we needed. If we thought it was the knife, we would have missed the point (so to speak). Rather, it was more evidence that there is much more going on here than what we see on the surface of things. It was as if angels got together and planned the entire knife surprise to demonstrate to us that our thoughts are connected, that we can tap into the same thought stream, that the universe loves to give us the desires of our hearts, that we are part of a vast, surging power network and here, *here* is a little glimpse of it. Michael Talbot, an authority on quantum physics calls us "dormant yogis."

I'm sure that you have found that my brain, like the brain of all human beings, has nine billion cells. The difference is, I knew it.

—Albert Einstein in a letter written to be read
after his death and the examination of his brain

HOW GRAND THE GIFT OF YOUR SWEET KISS

The soul of man is not conscious of its powers until it is enlightened by spirit. Therefore, to evolve and grow, man must learn how to use and develop his own soul forces.

—Johannes Brahms, 19th century
German composer

Everything you do and say sends out waves. If we could see these waves, they might look like the drawings we've all seen of sound waves. Like ripples in a pond after a stone has been dropped into it, your waves move out from you toward others. They may shimmer and undulate for miles before they lose intensity.

When Michael Jordan flies across the basketball court for a slam-dunk, he flies for all who see him. The thrill and mastery he demonstrates uplifts us all. The concentric ripples of excitement and wonder he produces travel out until the whole field house is ringing with the same intense amazement.

In the same manner, your own words and actions propel great gusts of vibrating waves. You may or may not hear the roar of a crowd reverberating back to you as athletes and rock stars do, but nonetheless your wavy oscillations travel out from you and have an impact on the mood, thoughts, and feelings of everyone near you. You are also having an effect on the cellular and quantum activity within and around those nearby.

It has been demonstrated with galvanic skin response machines attached to leaves, that plants respond with stress to our negative thoughts and critical voices. Just as dramatically, they respond positively to loving words and thoughts. This is quite obviously true for the children, pets, and other people in our lives as well, and even our homes, yards, and offices.

Certain highly sensitive people can actually feel the sound waves from harsh words, swearing, and unkind criticism. These ripples are jagged and full of intense penetrating energy. They can actually cause physical pain. When a child cries after a parent has yelled at him or her, they may actually be experiencing physical pain. If we could visually witness these sound waves we produce and how they move into another's space, we would be astounded at our power. It would be as if suddenly we realized our gun was loaded with real bullets when we thought it was loaded with blanks.

And let us consider as well the uplifting power of your grin, your wink, your friendly open-palm wave, your tender kiss, your words of encouragement, your expressions of love. How vast the power, how grand the gift you give! *And when you smile, the Great Holy Omnipresence of God is set free upon your face.*

> *...Mind is the builder. This refers to the Universal Mind of which each one of our minds is an individuated fragment. Mind, on all planes of existence, creates the pattern from which material things are formed.*
> —Edgar Cayce, 20th century American psychic healer

YOU ARE HEAVEN MADE TANGIBLE

> *Nothing can be taught to the mind which is not already concealed as potential knowledge in the unfolding soul.*
> —Sri Aurobindo, 20th century Indian yogi

We now know that some people who have been diagnosed with multiple personality symptoms can experience a change in a physical condition when they switch to a different personality. Such conditions as epilepsy and diabetes have been clinically diagnosed in one personality and then disappear when a different personality takes over. The symptoms of epilepsy and diabetes literally disappear in the other personality, even though the same body is being tested. Some people with multiple personalities even have to carry several different pairs of eyeglasses because their different personalities have different visual problems or none at all.

This suggests an awesome power in our brains and psyches to instantly change physical processes. It is quite likely that the same power is brought to bear in the many documented cases of instantaneous miracle healings.

Such miracles, for most of us, tend to take place on a less than conscious level. In general, most of us don't seem to be in total conscious control of our little manifestations and miracles. What we need to learn before we gain conscious access to all our power is that we do not force matter to conform to our will. Instead we learn to resonate or get in tune with the material and with the will of the Divine.

Each of us is a miniature universe, a tiny hologram that carries within it all the aspects of the entire universe. Thus, we carry within us the basic pattern for manifesting matter out of energy. As the earth glides into the visible out of the etheric realm, so our earthly bodies gain tangibility out of the etheric template of our soul's longing to play. The kingdom of heaven, *oh yes*, it is definitely within you.

YOU KNOW MORE THAN YOU KNOW

*Clear your mind of dogmatic
theological debris; let in the fresh,
healing waters of direct perception.
Attune yourself to the active inner*

> *Guidance; the Divine Voice has the answer*
> *to every dilemma of life. Though man's*
> *ingenuity for getting himself into trouble*
> *appears to be endless, the Infinite*
> *Succor is no less resourceful.*
> —Lahiri Mahasaya, 19th century Indian yogi, quoted by
> Paramahansa Yogananda

What is the kingdom of heaven? Surely a realm rich with power. Words may not be able to adequately describe it, but we can know it. How can we know a thing when we have no words for it? Because we can think holographically. Physicists and scientists are demonstrating the holographic properties of the mind. Once believed to be the province of yogis, saints and miracle workers, it is clear now that you and I have these same capacities. We think with words on a conscious level. That has been our conditioning. But, on a deeper level, we think holographically in symbols that capture a thousand words in an instant. Our dreams, replete with symbols, parables, riddles, and metaphors are but one of the many arenas in which our minds are set free to communicate beyond the limits of words.

Bob and Ann Nunley, pioneers in the human potential movement, teach a self-communication technique known as the "symbolic process". It is one of many new, yet ancient, ways we can all now use to discover who we are. Ann describes the process in detail in her recently published book *Inner Counselor:An Intuitive Guide for Life's Journey.*

I recall a woman named Sue who felt overwhelmed by a nameless sense of restriction and entrapment. Although she longed to express herself as a painter, she felt helpless to move past her compulsively orderly life which left no time or energy for art. In a symbolic process session, Sue closed her eyes and breathed deeply. Going deep within, with the assistance of a friend and her own higher self, she asked to "see" and talk to the feeling of restriction that so limited her.

The feeling appeared in her imagination looking like a suit of armor encasing her entire body. When she asked it what its good intentions were for her, it replied it had been with her since early childhood trying to keep her safe and make her feel strong and protected from the verbal abuse of her father. Moved by the sincerity of the suit of armor, Sue thanked the armor for working so hard to protect her all those years.

Then she explained to it that the imaginary, protective, warlike armor was feeling very restrictive. She expressed her desire to remove it in hopes that she would, then, feel more free and less restricted. Then, she asked her higher self to bring her a new symbol that could help keep her safe, as the armor had done, yet also give her courage to be more creative in her life.

While she watched with her mind's eye, her higher self appeared in her imagination as a beautiful woman, clothed in a flowing white robe. This loving higher self gently removed each piece of armor and piled the pieces together. As each bit of armor was taken off of her body, starting at her feet, Sue could feel new energy streaming into her body and tears of joy flowed freely at the heady sensation of liberation. It is amazing how the symbolic process works at such a deep emotional level. Even though there was no armor visible in the waking state, in the symbolic state, it felt very real to Sue. Thus, the removal of it caused a tremendous sense of relief.

At last, all the metal coverings were piled beside Sue. An image began to take shape at the horizon of her mind. What was it? Clouds billowed around shafts of sunlight and out of it came a magic carpet. Woven with ruby red and golden threads, it was alive with personality and enthusiasm. It flew to Sue as her heart pounded with excitement and a broad smile transformed her previously tense face. Following the steps of the symbolic process, Sue asked the pile of armor to allow the magic carpet to absorb all of the armor in order to incorporate, that is, fully embody the wise and loving intentions of the armor to protect her from harm. The shiny silver metal agreed and, as the carpet hovered above it, a thin thread of luminous silver spun out from the armor and wove itself into the tapestry of the carpet, making the carpet even stronger and more beautiful.

Finally, all the metal was transformed into thread and woven into the carpet. Through this great unraveling of stiffness and constriction came a new paradigm of freedom, adventure, and unlimited possibilities for Sue. After more than a year since this session and several others, Sue is convinced that this holographic symbolic process has helped her immensely.

It is through imagery techniques, such as this one, that people are accomplishing in a few sessions what used to take years of therapy. Why? Because we are learning to get in synch with our higher selves, our souls, our spiritual essence, and to communicate deeply beyond words. To bring spirit into matter and heaven into earth, heart must communicate with head; emotion and intuition must connect with intellect.

THE GRAND PARADOX: POWER'S INTIMATE DANCE WITH HELPLESSNESS

How can I say we are all blessed with power when all around us we see, or perhaps experience, the results of abuse, drunk drivers, corrupt dictators, civil wars, famine, hurricanes, plane crashes, fires, cancer, prejudice...? Once again I ask you to look with me at ourselves with bi-level awareness. On one level, as spiritual beings, we are the offspring of God who is All-the-Power-in-the-Universe. We are made of the Power of Love. It's as simple as that. That is our essence. Now, on the other level, we spirits are expressing ourselves through physical bodies and personalities. These bodies and personalities are subject to all sorts of accidents, traumas, and tragedies. The paradox is that as spiritual beings we are unbelievably powerful and as physical beings we often feel quite powerless and weak.

With bi-level awareness, it is possible to see how the two apparent opposites of power and weakness can work together to help us grow and know ourselves and to learn how to love. What is power after all? It is the drop of water that slowly, over thousands of years, wears away a huge granite stone, and, at the same time, it is Niagara Falls overwhelming our senses with rainbows and mist and thunder. It is the gentle hand that rocks the cradle, and, at the same time, it is the grown daughter or son running a multi-million dollar company. It is the executioner and, at the same time, it is the prisoner offering his executioner forgiveness. It is the wild, tearing, ripping tornado, and it is the gentle, healing breeze. You contain within you both the massive strength of the raging sea and the calming power of peaceful still waters.

The great success of Alcoholics' Anonymous and many other 12 step programs depends partly on two mind-boggling paradoxes. The first is that in order to remove pain, we must first endure pain.

I remember Tom who wanted the happiness he could have with his family, but his wife refused to let him live in their home until he got help for his alcoholism. Through AA meetings, he learned that, in order to have that happiness, he would first have to endure the pain of admitting he was an alcoholic and then live through the physical and mental agony of refusing to satisfy his addiction. No matter how much his body begged for alcohol, he would have to refuse it.

The pain of being separated from his family and his alcohol was so unbearable at one point that Tom impulsively grabbed his loaded shotgun and turned it, aiming at his own chest. He pulled the trigger, but some unseen force seemed to be pushing the barrel away from his chest. When the gun discharged, his left side was grazed, but he was alive. There he sat bleeding— and transformed. He knew deep within him that his guardian angel had prevented him from dying that day, and he could only conclude that there must be a reason. Through his hopelessness and helplessness, Tom found a greater strength than he had ever known. He never took another drink.

On a mythical or metaphorical level, Tom had to face his inner dragon in the cave of his unconscious. The dragon guarded the pot of gold that was Tom's treasure of inner spiritual strength. The dragon was the part of Tom that would appear to try to destroy him. Yet it was the dragon that provided

Tom with a way to exercise his own courage, to reach his treasure, to transform his life, gain self-respect, and contact his spiritual nature.

Another paradox that AA so beautifully reveals to us is that we gain power through admitting our powerlessness. The very first step of AA's 12 steps is this: "We admitted we were powerless over alcohol, that our lives had become unmanageable." The second step is: "We came to believe that a Power greater than ourselves could restore us to sanity." Through surrender and humility, paradoxically, we find a restoration of sanity, inner strength, and integrity.

Faith requires that we relinquish control and in the relinquishing, receive it back transformed. St. Francis of Assisi, who figured out how to synchronize power and humility, taught that it is in giving that we receive.

Powerlessness is the door we must open to discover the power of love on the other side. It is through loss that we find the power of mourning, and it is through the violation of human and animal rights that we are privileged to see the power of love outraged.

> *They that wait upon the Lord shall*
> *renew their strength; they shall*
> *mount up with wings as eagles; they*
> *shall run, and not be weary; and*
> *they shall walk and not faint.*
> —Bible: Isaiah 40:31

> *How could the rivers and the seas*
> *become like kings to valleys?*
> *Because of skill in lowliness, they*
> *have become the valley's lords.*
> —Lao Tzu, 7th century B.C. Chinese philosopher and
> founder of Taoism

EMBRACING THE PARADOX

I recall a story of an elderly woman who was brutally attacked by a would-be rapist in the women's restroom of a cafe.

Her screams went unheard in the noisy restaurant. Her kicking and fighting was no match for the big man's strength, but her prayers were something else again. As loudly as she could, she prayed to God to help her, over and over again. Finally, the man, flustered and confused by her feistiness in the face of his superior strength and bewildered by her stubborn faith, walked away mumbling "I believe in God too, and I need help..."

"Out of the mud, the lovely lotus"; out of weakness, strength; out of hatred, love; not 'instead of', but rather 'out of'. Weakness is not the opposite of strength after all, but instead the very filmy, vibrating edge from which power takes form.

The word 'sin' literally means 'missing the mark'. The main 'mark' that we're aiming for is a realization of who we are and who everyone else is. We keep forgetting that we are all sacred, holy, eternal spirits, because we get distracted and uni-level instead of bi-level in our vision. We see the physical world and forget that we are spirits only visiting earth in temporary physical bodies. Through the crucifixion and resurrection, Jesus wanted to save us from missing the mark, to awaken us from our spiritual amnesia.

Jesus's life and transfiguration was a metaphorical message to us. His message is this: that *we are all wounded healers*, exquisitely pierced by the knives and swords and dragons' teeth of earth life. With each wound, another pain is revealed to us, and our petals of compassion and healing and unconditional love unfold a little more. There is power in the blood of the Great Healer who consciously allows his body to be captured and 'killed' for the good of all. He is demonstrating to us that there is power in our blood, spirit in our matter, heaven in our earth. Holocaust survivors continue to wash the world with their blood and their tears, and with each story that is told, Love grows more bold.

Sometimes the difficulty may not so much be that we feel weak and powerless, but more that we are afraid of our own power. Power carries with it, not just images of wealth, prestige, and success, but also dictators and billionaires violating the rights of others. We all intuitively know that power without love and consciousness is frightening indeed. Therefore, to let loose the power within ourselves, when we are not yet fully cognizant of who we are, when we do not yet fully trust or know ourselves, is a bit unsettling. It is as if we have an inner corps of engineers that is constantly on the lookout for rivers to dam up in order to protect us from uncontrolled flooding and to use our power in steady, measurable amounts. But beneath the placid surface of the dammed lake, your wild river still runs.

I had a whole series of dreams over a month's time about birds in cages and free birds flying. I thought it meant I was trying to break free of something. Then one day, while I was journalling, I realized I was dreaming two parts of myself: the one that wants to be free of all restrictions and cages and the one that wants to belong somewhere, to be safe, and possessed, and adored. We are beings of paradox. We are light and dark; we are freedom and attachment; we are strength and weakness. Let us embrace our whole selves—not just the light and the free and the powerful and not just the dark, the lost, the weak and wounded. Let us embrace it all. For it is in defining ourselves as weak only that we neglect and fail to use our power; and it is in defining ourselves as powerful only that we become driven by the fear of losing that power.

We are all at once powerful and powerless, queens and slaves, free and imprisoned. We are explorers of all the ways we can be, deep seeing divers into the pools of our own essence. It is through our powerlessness that we learn compassion and yearn to surrender our will to God's will, and it is through our power that we align our will with God's will and commit compassionate acts.

Let us open our arms wide and welcome our whole selves, all our opposing traits, all our paradoxes, all our conflicting energies. Let us hold that tension and lay claim to both the lion and the lamb within us and refuse to polarize ourselves any longer, *and watch*. It is then, as we watch, that we feel the holy integration taking place, and, out of that, the humble warrior, the wounded healer steps forth.

Something opens our wings;
something makes boredom and hurt
disappear; someone fills the cup in
front of us; we taste only sacredness.
—Jalal ed-Din Rumi, 13th century Persian Sufi poet

Our deepest fear is not that we are
inadequate. Our deepest fear is that
we are powerful beyond measure...
We were born to make manifest the
glory of God that is within us. It's
not just in some of us; it's in every-
one. And as we let our own light
shine, we unconsciously give other
people permission to do the same. As
we are liberated from our own fear,
our presence automatically liberates others.
—Nelson Mandela, 20th century African leader

THE CHAKRA CONNECTION:
THIRD BLESSING—POWER
THIRD CHAKRA—POWER

May the blessing of power flow through you at the place in you where your third chakra vibrates. This is the solar plexus chakra or energy center located, of course, at the solar plexus area. This chakra is energetically associated with the stomach, liver, and adrenal glands. It is primarily concerned with having an effect on the external world, having a sense that we have some control over our lives.

Martial artists often locate the body's center of power at the third chakra. Body language specialists and our own intuition tells us that when we feel threatened, we often cross our arms protectively over our power center. When we feel powerful or want to appear very confident, we stand with hands on hips, body straight, solar plexus forward. Sometimes the simple act of strengthening the abdominal muscles can help us renew a sense of personal power.

Fear that we are being overpowered in some way can cause stomach upset, indigestion, and even nausea. If you have chronic pain or illnesses connected with the solar plexus area, including the adrenal glands, it's very possible that your body is talking to you. Since it is speaking to you from the power chakra, it is probably trying to tell you that your self-esteem and your sense of personal power are suffering. You are figuratively kicking yourself in the stomach with inner criticism. The interaction of your digestive system with any or even all food may be affected, because symbolically you are not nourishing your soul. Your body energetically responds to that, thus going unnourished itself.

May we all breathe in, deep down into our solar plexus, the Divine power of the universe. May we feel Creator dwelling in us there and filling us with tender humility and compassionate power.

EXPERIENCING THE BLESSING OF POWER

Make two lists. On one side of the page list five things about yourself that make you feel powerless or helpless, or you can list five times in your life when you felt helpless or powerless. On the other side of the page list five things about yourself that make you feel powerful and competent, or you can list five times in your life when you felt powerful and competent. Study the two lists and note any connections you see between them. You may be very surprised at what you discover about yourself.

Write a few paragraphs about your feelings or times of powerlessness. Describe how they helped you. For example, being gravely ill and feeling dependent on others may have helped you understand the needs of seriously ill people and other beings. Then, write about how your experiences of competence helped you.

Now, survey what you have written—these lists of qualities and events that help make you the unique, complex, and amazing person that you are. Close your eyes and imagine your higher self embracing all these aspects of you with love and compassion.

*Whatever you can do or dream you
can, begin it. Boldness has genius,
power, and magic in it.*

—Johann Wolfgang von Goethe, 18th
century German poet and scientist

A PRAYER

Oh, Mighty Warrior of the Universe

You have knighted us with your sword of Light. And while we yet bow before You, awe-filled at the nearness of your Power, You ask us to rise and walk with You. Imagine!

Are You saying that You trust us to do Your work; to be Your knights; to stand abreast with You facing all manner of fearsome and dangerous things? And are You saying that together with You we cannot fail to find the Holy Grail?

Help us to awaken, oh Lord of Lightning and Thunder and Nebulas and Tides. Help us to comprehend the fact that Your Divine Power runs through our veins and our souls, and guide us ever nearer to the Everlasting, ever-renewable source of that Power which is your Undying Love for us.

Om Amen Onne Ho

4th

BLESSING

YOU ARE LOVED

I love you without boundaries or limits. There is nothing as vast and infinite as My Love for you. There is nothing you can do that will dissuade Me from loving you. You are made of My Love, and nothing can separate us from each other.

The Blessing of Love

Loved on earth are we, and beyond that, throughout all eternity. We cannot escape the vast, infusing, enveloping Love that aches to hold each one of us in Endless Embrace.

> *There is a spirit which is mind and*
> *life, light and truth, and vast spaces.*
> *He contains all works and desires,*
> *and all perfumes and all tastes. He*
> *enfolds the whole universe, and in*
> *silence is loving to all.*
> —Rig Veda 11:28, Hindu Scriptures, 1500 B.C.

> *I saw that God never began to love*
> *us. We have always been in God's*
> *foreknowledge, known and loved*
> *from without beginning.*
> —Julian of Norwich, 14th century English mystic

We are God's gateways, *each one of us an arbor through which Divine Love may pass*, carrying with It your sweet scent and mine.

Our bodies are metaphors for our spirits. Mother Earth is a metaphor for Creator. Earth mother feeds our bodies and fills our lungs and teases our lips with the taste of fruit and honey and lovers' kisses. And just beyond and within such earthly matters, divinity breathes in and out, in and out. And we as *body, mind, and spirit* feel the rhythm, sense the synchrony of earth and heaven at play within us, seeking union, seeking creation, embracing, releasing, and making Love without end.

Even more than that, *we are an infinity of gateways*, every pore, every synapse, every cell and membrane, both our eyes, both our ears, our welcoming grins, our cradling arms. All these are doorways through which comes the invisible into the visible. The Word, the Breath, the Love of the Big Holy passes through the magic portal of you and suddenly becomes tangible.

Imagine how beautiful to see the ordinarily invisible pulsations of divinity entering and leaving your physical body. Imagine the white light of love entering your body through the top of your head. Then, like a prism refracting sunlight into the seven sacred colors: blue beams stream out from your fingertips when you reach out to comfort a friend; golden rays emanate from your face as you smile; violet cords extend miles and miles from you to a friend in your thoughts; and a ruby red stream flows from your heart whenever you speak a kind word.

And I would guess that whenever you look into your lover's eyes or cradle your child or feel at one with a tree, and if we could actually see all the colors and lights emanating from you in such ecstatic moments, it would be like gazing into the sun.

God's love passes through us all the time. Everything we do on earth in these bodies is an attempt, no matter how conscious or unconscious, no matter how clumsy or graceful, to deal with that powerful river of love running through us.

> *I have called Him [Christ] 'Light',*
> *but I could also have said 'Love',*
> *for that room was flooded, pierced,*
> *illuminated, by the most total com-*
> *passion I have ever felt. It was a*
> *presence so comforting, so joyous and*
> *all-satisfying that I wanted to lose*
> *myself forever in the wonder of it.*
> —George Ritchie, 20th century American
> physician commenting on his near death experience

YOU ARE IN THE HANDS OF THE BIG HOLY

> *And knowing God is not reserved*
> *for the great ones. It is for little*
> *folks like you and me. God is*
> *always seeking you—every one of you.*
> —Peace Pilgrim, 20th cent. American

As I prepared for my shower the other day, I saw a big, shiny, black ant wandering around by the drain. The sides of our tub were much too steep for him to climb. His life was in my hands. If I turned on the water, his fate would be sealed.

I found a piece of cardboard and proceeded to coax him aboard my little magic carpet. Mr. Ant could see no particular sense in cooperating with a giant so huge he could not even make out what I was, for certain. Finally, I had to trick him onto the cardboard and trap him with my hand so he would not leap off, preferring possible oblivion to whatever I was trying to do with him. Out of the tub he went and out into the yard to safety. I don't suppose he ever knew that I saved his little body from certain death.

Our Higher Power, our Divine, our Beloved watches over us this way. We may struggle to stay out of the path of the Giant Loving Hand that continually attempts to move us out of harm's way, but it is only because, with limited sight, we do not know where we are or how close to the drain we may be. Those who have actually seen the Giant know. We are all being lifted and loved, carried and cherished one at a time and all at once.

> *That voice is round me like a*
> *bursting sea;*
> *And is thy earth so marred,*
> *Shattered in shard on shard?*
> *Lo, all things fly thee, for thou*
> *fliest me!*
> *All which I took from thee I did but*
> *take, not for thy harms,*
>
> *But just that thou might'st seek it*
> *in my arms.*
> *All which thy child's mistake fancied*
> *as lost, I have stored for thee*
> *at home.*
> *Rise, clasp my hand, and come!*
> —Francis Thompson, 19th century poet

> *Like God's wide net enclosing all,*
> *Its mesh is coarse but none are lost.*
> —Lao Tzu, 600 B.C. Chinese philosopher
> and founder of Taoism

GOD'S PASSIONATE ATTACHMENT TO YOU

> *Yours is the Heaven that lies in the*
> *common dust, and You are there for*
> *me, You are there for all.*
> —Rabindranath Tagore, 19th and 20th century Indian writer
> and teacher

It is human to long for romance. And it is also divine. That longing is a deep, compelling need to bring to earth the heavenly oneness our souls remember and to bring divine love into earthly form. We are beings of love. How many songs do you suppose have been written around the world about falling in love, being in love, and losing our love? Is it a worldwide, mass mind obsession? No—it is our mission. We have come here to unite heaven and earth and to bring the Love that we *are* into Be-ingness. We are Love seeking Love everywhere and trying to remember that we already have what we seek.

In that first entrancing moment when first we do believe our lover loves us perfectly and we, in our embrace, are lost to earth, there is nothing in all the world except our love. That moment forever has a taste and scent that we will always know and recognize. It is this language of the holy embrace that is our native tongue, and when we rest in it, we know that we are home. Just as ocean waves roll on to a sandy beach and penetrate the sand with wetness, love rolls over us and changes us forever.

When we fall in love or bond with someone, one of the things we often say is that we could not bear to be separated from one another. How it lifts our spirits to know that we are desperately needed by another, that our living is intensely important to someone else. Indeed, our love may feel so powerful that we simply cannot imagine being lost to each other. We cannot bear the thought of our beloved leaving or dying.

God has all the attributes of Lover, Father, Mother, and Child. With Infinite Fondness, Desperate Adoration, and Passionate Attachment, we are held fast to our Beloved. We can never be lost, never be separated from that great Love-That-Is-In-All. Wallace Black Elk, a Lakota shaman, sometimes speaks of God as "Grandmother" and tells us that Her love for us is endless.

> *While everything is silent and asleep*
> *...I live at the feet of my God, pouring*
> *out my heart in love of Him, telling*
> *Him I love Him, while He tells me I*
> *shall never love Him as much as He*
> *loves me, however great my love may be.*
> —Father Charles de Foucauld, 20th century French
> missionary

> *Jesus has chosen to show me the only*
> *way which leads to the divine*
> *furnace of love; it is the way of*
> *childlike self-surrender, the way of*
> *a child who sleeps, afraid of nothing*
> *in its father's arms.*
> —St. Therese of Lisieux, 19th century French Catholic saint

THE WILD AND HOLY MYSTICAL ROMANCE

> *Devotees of all the ages, approaching the*
> *Mother in a childlike spirit, testify*
> *that they find Her ever at play with them.*
> —Paramahansa Yogananda, 20th century yogi

In the Hebrew language, the word for 'compassion' is derived from the word 'womb'. El Shaddai—one of the many Hebrew names for God—means "many breasted one". Among many religions of the native people of Africa, ancient Europe, Polynesia, the Americas, and Asia, there are many references to the Creator as a loving mother. The Big Holy, Great Spirit, Divine Goddess, Almighty God is our Divine Mother. And in the silence we can feel Her gently rocking us.

And, yes, this same Almighty Lord of Lords, King of Kings is our Heavenly Father. And in quiet moments we may see His outstretched hands beckoning us to take our next step.

Many are the saints and mystics who have spoken of their cosmic, mystical union with the Divine Lover. Saint Theresa of Avila, a 16th century saint of Spain, assured us all that our Lover constantly longs for communion with us and waits breathlessly for us to ask for the passionate, infilling embrace of Infinite Love. It is in the ecstatic moments of the Mystical Romance that people through the ages have realized the truth, *we are truly adored with a most Holy and Wild Abandon.*

RIDING THE WAVE OF LOVE

> *I felt as if I were the only person who appreciated being alive. I wanted to shake others, to tell them to take hold of their lives and live in joy in the fullness of this wonderful gift. I realized I hadn't been living each day to its capacity. I would never again take for granted each morning sunrise. I would never forget that every breath I took was a gift from God.*
> —Michelle Hamilton after being rescued from a tiny boat lost for many days at sea.

According to scientist Greg Braden, the emotion of fear, when recorded as a wave, is long and slow. Love, on the other hand, comes out as a shorter wave. Feelings are vibrations and, therefore, have vibratory patterns. These patterns can hold feelings in the body for many years and even contain them in certain organs. Greg believes there is a sacred circuit of vibrations that runs through earth to the heart, then to the brain, and then to the cells of our bodies, connecting all these to each other.

Perhaps, this is another way of describing the streaming of God's Love Energy through us. And if that love is a shorter more frequently pulsating wave, and if it is always there pulsing through our blood streams and our neural pathways, then let us believe that we can synchronize our souls with those love waves, and let the tide of fear move out and away to its own long, slow rhythm.

Oh Lord of Love, overtake us and dance with us to the heartbeat of Heaven and Earth.

> *Master, I saw Your face...I looked*
> *upon Your beauty. How shall I*
> *speak of what is unspeakable...but*
> *oh what movements of fire! Oh what*
> *swirlings of the flame in me coming*
> *from You and Your glory.*
> —Symeon, 10th century theologian

> *Love is continually bubbling up in*
> *them [people in communion with*
> *God]...it reminds me of little springs*
> *which I have seen gushing up and*
> *which keep on incessantly stirring*
> *up the sand all around them.*
> —St. Theresa of Avila, 16th century Spanish Catholic saint

THE GRAND PARADOX: LOVE'S INTIMATE DANCE WITH HATE

> *The first outburst of everything*
> *God does is compassion.*
> —Meister Eckhart, 13th/14th century mystic

> *... neither death, nor life, nor angels,*
> *nor principalities, nor powers, nor*
> *things present, nor things to come,*
> *nor height, nor depth, nor any other*
> *creature, shall be able to separate*
> *us from the Love of God, which is*
> *in Christ Jesus our Lord.*
> —Paul the Apostle, Romans 8:38, 39

The opposite of the fourth blessing that is paradoxically contained within it is hate.

All matters of concern eventually come to rest here within this paradox. All our journeys are treasure hunts seeking the reward of love. Yet all along the way we run into barbed wire barricades of hate and its progenitor—fear.

First and foremost is our own self-hatred. That self-hate lunges at us periodically out of the secret, dark places of shame and guilt within us that we fear so much and try so hard to deny. The paradox is this—it is not until we uncover our own self-hate and negotiate with it face to face that we are able to embrace ourselves and find our wholeness and our holiness. Then, in finding that, we discover the treasure: *our oneness, our calming inclusion with the whole, holy, infinitely loving universe.*

We are all here to learn how to love others and ourselves. It's as simple as that. Everything we do and everything done to us is a lesson about love. If we can remember what class we're taking here, then it's easier to make sense of all the Great Professor's parables and metaphors, synchronicities and challenges.

Our spirits talk to us of love. Quite capable are they of seeing the beauty, the divine in all creation, and most especially our loved ones. When we fall in love, spirit calls to body and, with a gentle dip of the wand, body is captivated at the sight of the radiant creature before it. The knees tremble; the heart beats faster; everything in sight gains a new brilliance, an effervescence not normally seen on earth. With our senses properly opened in this way, we, as spiritual beings, suddenly see life as it really is, in all its intensity. We see our beloved ones as they truly are: *pure, perfect, divine, and unbearably beautiful.* The veil that is usually trailing and billowing between ourselves and others is gone when we fall in love. We are privileged to view our lovers as angels and mothers do. We see them glowing and pulsing with the inner light of which they are truly made.

There is talk that this condition is a spell cast upon us when we first fall in love, and that over time, we revert to a more realistic perception. In fact, what actually happens is that we revert to an unrealistic perception and can no longer see the true nature, true face, true soul in those bright eyes that we once accurately perceived. The veil drapes its folds between us, and we look through at a gauzy reminder of the lover once so dazzling.

If we do fall from grace in each other's eyes, it is because we wage war within ourselves as we attempt to reach impossible ideals. Not being at peace with ourselves, we find it difficult to be at peace with our lovers. Our conflicts draw more veils down between us and narrow our field of view. Sometimes those we love the most even take the appearance of enemies.

And what would a discussion of hate be without mention of the truly hateable and dangerous—the rapists, serial killers, evil dictators, torturers? It is truly challenging to talk of a world full of love and made of love when these people exist and continue to threaten others.

> *There is no difficulty that enough*
> *love will not conquer...*
> —Emmet Fox, 20th century American minister

EMBRACING THE PARADOX

> *When I speak of love...I am speaking*
> *of that force which all of the great*
> *religions have seen as the supreme*
> *unifying principle of life. Love is*
> *somehow the key that unlocks the*
> *door which leads to ultimate*

> *reality. This Hindu-Moslem-*
> *Christian-Jewish-Buddhist [and this*
> *author would add Native] belief about*
> *ultimate reality is beautifully*
> *summed up in the first epistle of*
> *Saint John: Let us love one another;*
> *for love is God.*
> —Martin Luther King, 20th century American spiritual leader
> and minister

At the end of World War II, soldiers arrived at one of the concentration camps to relocate the many prisoners. One of the prisoners seemed to be in excellent condition and was helping the soldiers with their work. They assumed he must have been captured fairly recently to have been in such good condition and high spirits. Imagine their amazement when they learned he had been there for six years. His entire family had been shot by the soldiers who imprisoned him. He told his liberators: "I had seen too often what hate could do to people's minds and bodies. Hate had just killed the six people who mattered most to me in the world. I decided then that I would spend the rest of my life—whether it was a few days or many years—loving every person I came in contact with."

It is my wish to help you feel the ecstasy of remembering who you really are. Observe your chest as you hold this book. See it rise and fall as you breathe in and out. Who is watching the breathing? Who is breathing? Feel where you are. You are the observer. You have a body that breathes. You have a personality that has quirks and talents and repressed rage and generosity, and you can observe all that. *You are pure, holy awareness.* You are essential spirit. You are your higher self—*God's dear companion and artful co-creator.*

The more fully we are able to identify with and know we are, indeed, this pure spirit observer self, then the more we are free to embrace and nurture the immature parts of ourselves and help them to transform. With the power and freedom generated by this deep romance with ourselves, we become more and more liberated to love others and all our relations unconditionally.

The secret to falling in love with yourself is this: In the words of Eva Pierrakos, a brilliant spiritual teacher, "...the moment you acknowledge the heretofore unacceptable [aspect of yourself], you cease to be the unacceptable and instead you are identified with that in you that is capable of the acknowledgment."

In other words—face what it is about your personality or your actions that you find unacceptable. These could be very obvious to you, or they could be repressed memories that will surface only with gentleness and time. Talk about these, describe them, cry about them, mourn what must be mourned, and through it all recall again and again—you are the observer here. You are the healer, the loving counselor to your own body and personality. As you can, and as you identify with your observer self, it becomes easier to relinquish your previous harsh judgment of yourself, to actually step into your higher self and be there. And being there, right there standing in your spirit, in your authentic being—turn and gaze with adoration at the physical you, with the eyes of an enchanted lover. If only for this moment, let yourself fall helplessly in love with you. Let love sweep you off your feet for you. *You are so beautiful.*

This is where it all begins. This is the tasting, the romancing, the pyrotechnic display of love set free. For each time we are able to let go of self-judgment and grasp the significance of our own elegant *love-liness*, then—how delicious and sweet-scented and worthy and sacred All Creation becomes for us.

Perhaps, all art, even all expression, is an attempt at self-healing, an attempt to find wholeness in our seemingly fractured and fragmented psyches. A woman in our town recently had a triumphant art show displaying two years' worth of exquisite paintings. Pinned to the wall beside one of her masterpieces was her humble note that she had created this art during a period of severe depression. This outward expressing in inks and oils of what had for so long tumbled about within her had helped her revive her zest for life. A friend of mine writes passionately unnerving fiction nearly every day. He feels that if he did not get it out of his head and onto paper, it would be like dammed up water with nowhere to go.

Yet her paintings and his writings are much more than

healing activities for themselves. These wounded healers are offering to the world the flowers that have bloomed in the caverns of their pain.

My wounds, self-inflicted and otherwise, like yours, are too numerous to count. Many things have happened in our lives that we cannot change. Yet it is through the deepest wounds that we find the most penetrating love. The idea is not so much to heal the wound as it is to feel the love that comes to us because we are wounded and then to find a way to pass that love on.

Through my pain, you are healed; through your pain, I am healed. And the healing circles round and round 'til one day the spinning vortex of love and grace becomes so visible to us that we can "see" the Love-That-We-Are-In.

The paradox reveals that hatred bears a priceless gift. Hatred comes to us and says: "I come to you continually to make you hungry for the sweet taste of love, until your hunger drives you steadfast and ever more into Love's waiting arms. Then my service to you will be done."

> *...All creatures as children of God*
> *hold compassion in common.*
> *Divinity is not outside us. We are in*
> *God and God is in us. That is the*
> *unitive experience of mystics east*
> *or west.*
> —Matthew Fox, 20th century American theologian

THE CHAKRA CONNECTION:
FOURTH BLESSING—LOVE
FOURTH CHAKRA—HEART

May the blessing of love flow through you at the place in you where your fourth chakra vibrates. The fourth chakra is generally thought and felt to be located in the center of the chest around the heart area. Energetically it is connected to the heart and the circulatory system. It is usually referred to as the heart chakra. The issues that the heart chakra deals with are love and compassion for others as well as ourselves.

Symbolically and energetically, the lower three chakras are related primarily to issues of physical survival. The first chakra of survival relates to staying alive; the second chakra of relationships relates to finding protection by belonging to a group; and the third chakra of power is all about empowering ourselves to deal with the physical realm.

The upper three chakras, that is, the 5th, 6th, and 7th, have traditionally been considered to be more concerned with spiritual issues. The heart chakra, being directly in between the upper three and lower three, is thought to be the meeting point of spirit and body, the marriage bed where heaven and earth unite within us.

It is through the passage of the heart that our life blood flows out to our upper and lower extremities and then back to the heart. Let us sit quietly for a few moments and listen to our hearts. Let us hear and feel the rhythmic pumping. The heart does not hang onto the blood for fear of losing it. It pumps it out rich with oxygen and nutrients to all the limbs and tissues and organs in perfect faith that it will all return in perfect time. And pumping out leads naturally to drawing in. They are two steps in the same dance.

In the same manner, when we open our hearts and send out love on the outbeat, love is drawn back in to us on the inbeat. Let us drink a deep breath of life and send it to our heart chakras. Let us feel our hearts overflowing with God's tender love for us. Let us close our eyes and imagine our higher selves walking ceremoniously toward us. Imagine you as your own true, beautiful higher self placing a gentle, strong hand on your body's chest and blessing your heart with overflowing love.

> *If you wish to discipline the flesh,*
> *then put on it the bridle of Love.*
> *Whoever has accepted the sweet burden*
> *of the bridle of Love will attain more*
> *and come much further than all the*
> *penitential practices and mortifications*
> *that all the people in the world acting*
> *together could ever carry out.*
> —Meister Eckhart, 14th century German theologian and mystic

EXPERIENCING THE BLESSING OF LOVE

1. Make two columns on a sheet of paper. The first column will be headed "things I really dislike about myself." The second column is titled "things I really like or love about myself."

Example:

Things I dislike or hate

I'm shy in crowds

I didn't try harder to save
    my marriage

Things I like or love

I give lots of compliments

I'm a hard worker

When you are finished, step back. Imagine gazing at the lists from the being of your higher self, your spirit that lives beyond time and space and beyond and within your body and personality. Be your higher self. Feel the Love of the Universe pouring through your spirit as you gaze affectionately at the lists your personality has written. Notice that, as pure spirit, you cannot see anything but perfection and beauty in your earth-being. You feel filled with compassion and love for this totally unique you. From the heart of your higher self, embrace the totality of the lists, both the things disliked and the things loved about yourself. Allow the feeling of Divine Total Acceptance to bless your heart.

2. You may want someone to read this to you as you sit quietly and breathe deeply.

There is a point of light within you. I want you to imagine this point of light right near your heart. Picture it with your mind or feel it—a small, shining starlight in the center of your being. You feel the warmth coming from it. You see its radiance. It is so beautiful. It is alive with light and warmth. Spend a moment just enjoying that light. (Pause a moment to give your listener time to imagine the light.)

Now, I am going to speak some messages from the Creator to you. As I speak these messages, I want you to see or feel the words as if they were appearing in soft, white, cloud-like letters written in the deep blue sky of your mind. As I speak the words slowly, I want you to breathe deeply and inhale the words. Then, hold your breath, and let the words come to rest in your heart where the light is. Then, I want you to exhale and leave the words behind, written on your heart. As you do this, you will sense the light growing brighter and warmer and filling your entire being with joy and peace.

Here is the first phrase. Listen to the words. Picture them in your mind or feel them if you have trouble visualizing them. When I finish, breathe deeply and experience the words going deep into your being.

My Child, I love you without boundaries or limits. (Be silent for a minute or two as the listener allows these words to comfort him or her.)

Here is the second phrase. Listen. Picture the letters of each word forming. Breathe in the words. Then, hold your breath for a moment and allow the words to come to rest in your heart where the light is. Then, when you are ready, exhale, leaving the words behind written on your heart.

My Child, there is nothing as vast and infinite as My love for you. (A minute of silence follows.)

Here is the third phrase. Remember to breathe in the words, hold them in your heart as you hold your breath a moment, then leave them with your heart as you exhale.

My Child, there is nothing you can do that will dissuade Me from loving you. (A minute of silence follows.)

Here is the fourth phrase. Hold it in your heart.

My Child, you are made of My love, and nothing can separate us from each other. (A minute of silence follows.)

Now, as you return to your waking state, take a deep breath and know that God loves you and is always with you to comfort you and give you peace. Know that these words are all true and always true for you.

A PRAYER

Father God, Mother Goddess

Help us to dive into our divinity and fully receive all the love of the universe which is continually being poured out to us and all beings.

Help us to see how You love us through stars and people and animals and all our relations.

Help us to feel the trees blessing us as we pass beneath their branches.

Help us to stop our struggle to cling to love. Help us to know that we cannot lose that of which we are made. Every day we drink from Your Fountain of Youth, from Your Holy Grail, from Your Spring of Living Water—all day long.

Thank you for patiently, endlessly passing us the cup; for nourishing us with Your Unconditional Love. And when we fall—too weak to hold the cup—You hold us to Your breast, until we can grow once again from Holy Infant to Blessed Child. You, who have borne us out of Immaculate Vapor and gaze at us with wonder in Your adoring eyes; You it is we thank for this all nourishing, endless Love.

Om Amen

5th

BLESSING

YOU ARE CREATIVE

Together you and I are Co-Creators. We birth energy into matter, light into form, Heaven into Earth, vibration into song. With every child you comfort, every stroke of your pen, every word from your lips and every kiss, you fill the universe with more beauty, more mystery, and more Love.

The Blessing of Creativity

Jesse Roberts went spear fishing one evening near the Fiji Islands. Walking in the shallow water off the island of Leleuvia, he strayed too far off the beach and was caught in the rising tide. No longer able to wade, he swam, but heavy waves and current began carrying him out into the open sea. Three times he reached exhaustion and slipped under the water expecting to drown. Each time, he felt lifted to the surface. The third time, after a desperate prayer to Jesus, he heard a voice say to him: "You are going on with my endurance. I have a plan for your life." Divinely guided and strengthened, he swam twelve miles in the dark to the island of Moturiki and lived to tell his story.

If you are reading this page right now, then you are alive in this material realm, just like Jesse. How long ago did you feel you were drowning? Perhaps, you've been gasping for breath beneath endless waves of bills, or perhaps, you have felt helplessly carried away by an overwhelming current of responsibilities, stress, or bad luck.

And yet you are still here, still breathing. Why? Because there is a Divine plan designed particularly for you, and you're not finished with it yet. We may not hear an audible voice as Jesse did in his state of dire emergency, but the fact that we are here now is incontrovertible proof that we need to be here, now, right where we are.

When we wake up in the morning and stretch and yawn and feel our fingers and toes filling back up with consciousness, and our brains slowly let go of the dream world and neurons begin firing in beta time, *witness the miracle*. Let us feel that same power of God that Jesse felt. Let us arise and go on with Divine Endurance. Let us rejoice, for each one of us has special reasons for being here. God has a plan for our lives. We are on sacred journeys. Let us travel on in trust.

> *The Sufis recognize God in all things.*
> *To them the desires for accomplish-*
> *ment...which one feels are expressions*
> *of the Divine impulse.*
> —Pir Vilayat Khan, 20th century Sufi master

> *We form God's presence in the world*
> *through the indwelling of His spirit.*
> —Paul Brand, surgeon and author with Philip Yancey, 20th century American writer

YOU ARE NEVER NOT CREATING

> *We should think of life as the accu-*
> *mulation of treasures. Every new*
> *friend made, every new truth*
> *learned or experience undergone*
> *makes us richer than we were.*
> —Rabbi Harold Kushner, 20th century American Jewish Rabbi

> *Do not pursue spectacular deeds.*
> *What matters is the gift of yourself,*
> *the degree of love that you put into*
> *each one of your actions.*
> —Mother Teresa, 20th century Catholic nun

Very well, we are creative beings, here on a mission from God. But how do we know what the mission is? How do we know what we're supposed to create?

First of all, may we admit that we are never not creating. Even in our sleep, we are creating visions, weaving complex tales, and solving problems.

Let us not underestimate, for example, what immeasurable treasure is loosed upon the earth by the simple creative act of remembering someone's birthday or cheering up a weary checker at the grocery store. Creativity is not confined to paintings, symphonies, and sculpture. Our lives are gilt-framed masterpieces; our relationships are performance art; our words—all notes and rhymes in the song of life and we—we are the composers.

Scientific experiments have shown that the human voice can change brain waves and blood pressure. Our voices produce complex wave forms. We can create peace and harmony with a single phrase, gently spoken. So we are creators, not now and then, but all the time.

Yet, comforting as that may be, still there seems to be in each of us a yearning to create more. Something calls us to yet more specific colors and tones and asks us to make even clearer footprints. The Creative Energy of All-That-Is flows through us all the time, but guilt and anger and fear can block that energy from flowing through.

Susan had what she thought was a crazy dream to be a professional singer. She discounted it for many years, because she believed she wasn't capable or talented enough. She attracted people, including two husbands, who compounded her already low self-esteem with critical and discouraging remarks. It wasn't until she joined a spiritual support group that she came to understand it was all right, even good, to love and appreciate herself. Slowly and step by step she gave herself permission to fall in love with Susan and to be thankful for who she was and what she had. As she did, to her surprise, her crazy dream, lying dusty in a forgotten closet of her mind, began to call to her. Some years later, she dared to act on her fantasy and actually became a professional singer.

God wants to take the cross of guilt and self-doubt off of our backs and lay it at our feet, making for us a cross-road. Oh Loving Creator—point the way.

In all thy ways acknowledge Him
and He shall direct thy paths.
—Holy Bible, Proverbs 3:6

I, God, am your Playmate! I will
lead the child in you in wonderful
ways for I have chosen you. Beloved
child, come swiftly to me, for I am
truly in you.
—Mechtild of Magdeburg, 13th century activist, mystic

DISCOVERING YOUR SACRED MISSION

The world is as you dream it...Come
learn to dream of beauty.
—Shuar tribal elder, 20th century, Native South American

We are co-creators with the Big Holy Creator of All Creation. We're in good company. We are not asked to get out of
God's way, but rather to put our minds, hearts, and souls together with the Creative Force of the Universe. This Force is
Pure Light, Energy, and Love aching for embodiment. It needs
each one of us to stir it all together in our own unique way and
show it forth.

Can you feel the Creator nudging you into creative partnership? Or do you feel distant and isolated from the Creative
Flame? Fear of failure, fear of social condemnation, fear of re-
jection—all these create the illusion of that distance and muffle
or distort the voice of our own truth. The Great Spirit, Universal Intelligence has inscribed our missions in our bones, our
genes, our connective tissue, our chakras, our very souls. Deep
within each of us is a mother lode of golden ideas waiting to be
brought out into the sunlight.

If we follow the treasure maps of others and neglect the
vein of gold within us, we may wander Death Valley a long
time.

Listen to your whole, holy self. Listen to your heart
quicken when you open to a certain idea. Feel the energy in
your knees and thighs charge up when you consider a certain
direction. Sense the passion in your soul come alive when you
admit what you really long for. *Trust.*

Perhaps, it seems you have spent too many years walking too carefully through the mine fields of other people's expectations. Yet, no matter how many years have passed, there is no loss, no mistake. All the insights and talents you have gained along the way will serve you well. Every experience we have, whether favored or not, helps us learn, refine, inform, and manifest who we really are.

> *...Live without a why, love without*
> *a why and work without a why.*
> —Meister Eckhart, 13th and 14th century
> German theologian and mystic

> *When you choose to make doing what*
> *you love the core experience in your*
> *life, you move into alignment with the Universe.*
> —Arnold Patent, 20th century American author

FINDING YOUR PASSION

> *The bird does not sing because he has*
> *an answer. The bird sings because he has a song.*
> —Author unknown

We are all turning and circling and sniffing and pawing like a wolf searching out the best spot for a nap. It's got to be a good place. It's got to smell right. It's got to feel safe. It's got to hold the promise of dreams about running free as the wind, smelling every scent, and following the scent that smells the best.

We are seeking ecstasy, not just of the flesh, and not just of the spirit, but ecstasy of both, where they meet—at the heart. My son's dog, Brook, knows that pure bliss is going for a run, simple as that. The look on her face, when it's time to run is it—that's the look—*pure unbridled passion and perfect focus*, every muscle taut and ready; eyes bright; bounding joy and enthusiasm in every bounce and every leap. There she goes!

Take a deep breath and recall some times in your life when your eyes shone as brightly as Brook's with the pure ecstasy of the moment. What is happening in those scenes? Breathe life back into those moments in your life. Let them carry you for a few more minutes, and see where they take you. Listen.

The word enthusiasm literally means "filled with God." The feeling of enthusiasm is—God set free within us to dance in our bodies and spark and vibrate in our brains. When we feel such enthusiasm or bliss, we are in harmony with God. We are feeling that synchrony, that mind-meld, that heart-meld between us and the Divine. Just as pain in your arm is a signal that you should stop and check it out and give it time to heal, bliss in your spirit is your signal to check out what you are doing that is bringing this bliss. It is a signal that you are close to your own particular soul's purpose.

> *Let yourself be silently drawn by*
> *the stronger pull of what you really love.*
> —Jalal ed-Din Rumi, 13th century Persian poet

THE TREASURE OF LIFE IS WITHIN YOU

> *One loving blind desire for God alone*
> *is...more helpful to your friends both*
> *living and dead, than anything else you can do.*
> —Unknown author of the *Cloud of Unknowing*,
> 14th century mystic

Lest you feel saddened by a lack of focus and passion in your life, consider this. Your journeys through your dark nights are also creative acts. Perhaps, these are the most courageous and creative acts of all. For, when we plod on, in the midst of hopelessness, with only the tiniest faith that we can somehow find happiness, we are creating from the very farthest reaches of our souls.

Often, before you can claim your birthright of bliss, you must prove yourself to yourself. This is the mythical hero's journey that we all must take. It is an ancient process of deliberately waking up and leaving behind the familiar. It is going into the dark forest of your deepest fears, hatreds, doubts, and despair. It is facing, with trembling heart, the witches and dragons that reside there, passing their various tests so that you can get past them unharmed. Then, when that is finished, when you have passed the tests and proven yourself to yourself, that is when you finally find the treasure and make the remarkable discovery that—*Aah the treasure is you.*

You discover the magic secret, hidden for so long in the dragon's dark cave—You are God's treasure, a sacred, holy, created creator; loved beyond all imagining, one with the Golden Streaming River of Universal Love which never stops flowing.

> *For where your treasure is, there*
> *your heart will be also.*
> —Jesus Christ, Luke 12:34

YOU ARE A MIRACLE MAKING MIRACLES

> *What then was the commencement*
> *of the whole matter? Existence*
> *that multiplied itself for sheer*
> *delight of being and plunged into*
> *numberless trillions of forms so that*
> *it might find itself innumerably.*
> —Sri Aurobindo, 19th and 20th century Indian nationalist
> leader and mystic philosopher

All creatures, all forms, all stars, indeed, all manifestations in the universe are miraculous creations of the Divine Artist. As such, our physical bodies are all made of sacred material and imbued with the energy of Creativity Itself. This energy flows through us and through all our relations—the stones, trees, plants, animals, planets, and seas. Let us touch a stone, a branch, a stem, a furry paw; feel the salty spray of sea; smell the leafy forest floor; feel the subtle heartbeat of our earth; hear our own heart beating. She moves through us and all life continually—this ancient and timeless, fierce and passionate, Mother giving birth to the Immaculate Divine in us all.

> *If one advances confidently in the direction of his dreams...He will put something behind, will pass an invisible boundary; new, universal, and more liberal laws will begin to establish themselves around and within him, or the old laws will be expanded and interpreted in his favor in a more liberal sense; and he will live with the license of a higher order of beings.*
> —Henry David Thoreau, 19th century American philosopher and poet

YOU CREATE TIME & SPACE

> *What is prayer but a form of thought transmission? By means of it you can draw upon the power of the divine mind where all wisdom reposes. Prayer is actually a line of communication along which come insights, intuitions, fresh understandings. With two calm minds working on a problem—God's mind and your mind—you're in.*
> —Norman Vincent Peale, 20th century American minister

Science continually fuels our growing understanding of who we are. Physicist David Bohm teases us with this idea: that each one of us has a brain that can construct space and time as well as construct reality out of frequencies that exist beyond time and space. We are connected to, or rather are an intrinsic part of the whole, holy hologram of Life Itself. When we consciously tune into these frequencies, we get into synch with the Cosmos; and the Cosmos is very, very creative.

> *Dwell as near as possible to the*
> *channel in which your life flows.*
> —Henry David Thoreau, 19th century American philosopher

> *Know you what it is to be a child?*
> *...it is to be so little that the elves*
> *can reach to whisper in your ear.*
> *It is to turn pumpkins into coaches,*
> *and mice into horses, lowness into*
> *loftiness and nothing into every-*
> *thing—for each child has his fairy*
> *godmother in his own soul. It is to*
> *live in a nutshell and count your-*
> *self king of the infinite space; it is*
> *to see the world in a grain of sand,*
> *Heaven in a wild flower,*
> *To hold infinity in the palm of your*
> *hand and eternity in an hour.*
> —William Blake, 18th century English poet

THE GRAND PARADOX: CREATION'S INTIMATE DANCE WITH DESTRUCTION

> *Listen, o drop, give yourself up*
> *without regret, and in exchange*
> *gain the ocean.*
> —Jelaluddin Rumi, 13th century, Sufi mystic

We are infinite beings who yet experience death. We are one with the universe, and yet we know loneliness intimately. We hold the power of the heavens, and yet we fear our own helplessness. We are beloved and capable of love beyond all our dreams, and still we may feel hatred and violence within us. We are many faceted in our wholenesses.

God gives us a mission of significant challenge, an affectionate dare—*that we love our whole selves—all that we contain, all that we are.* As we become more conscious and awake, we light up all the dark corners of hatred and loneliness and fear within us that we haven't wanted to see. In this way, we lighten up as we unload the burdens of guilt and fear, and we *en*lighten our hearts and minds.

With this lightening and this awakening consciousness of who we really are comes a greater dexterity with our blessings. That is to say, we can use them more deliberately and more serenely. With greater self-acceptance and self-love comes genuine love and acceptance for others and for all life.

The dark corner of creativity is what appears to be its opposite—destruction. But is it really an opposite? Creation is in a constant state of choosing. In order to create one thing, another must be carved away, burned off, painted over, or eliminated.

I am in the library today sitting by a floor to ceiling glass window. Behind me are thousands of books. Authors, publishers, artists, photographers, and scientists all took part in creating these books. Out beyond the window I see an asphalted intersection, six traffic signs, our town park decorated with colorful flowerbeds, a gazebo, and a winding sidewalk full of joggers, cyclists, families, and pets. Thousands of peoples' hands and minds created these things—carpenters, road builders, landscapers, sign makers, concrete artisans, architects, city planners, city tax payers.

And this is not all I see in this tiny patch of this little town. I see people in all kinds of clothing. I see electric, phone, and cable wires, a fire hydrant, bicycles, cars, and trees. Literally uncountable acts of creativity produced what I see in this one small area alone. Nearly everywhere we look we are undeniably surrounded by clear evidence of our natural state as creators. Our television sets are cornucopias of human creations spilling out an endless supply of ideas, products, laugh lines, and dramas.

Yet each creation, like us, carries within it the shadow or

the side we don't like to look at. Yet we must if we are to fully embrace our true nature as creatives and as co-creators with the Divine. That shadow is this—it is all that we choose to cover or destroy in order to create. In the scene I described, what was lost? Untraceable acres of trees for paper and lumber, nests, animal dens, the animals themselves, water purity, air quality, the sounds of nature.

On a very tiny scale, a songbird destroys a few twigs and grasses to make a nest, but it is so small we don't think of it as destruction. When, instead, millions of much larger humans need much bigger nests made out of trees instead of twigs, the line between creativity and destruction can get blurry.

And our creative urges are not slowing down. Instead, the pulse of human productivity seems to be escalating exponentially. We seem to be artists running out of canvas and paint. We are divine and eternal beings. At our very core, we are creators filled with the same passion for bringing spirit into matter as our own Creator. We, as Spirits, are beings not bound by time and space. Our creations, on the other hand, at least in their current form, exist in the space-time continuum. Our own bodies, the bodies of animals and plants, and all our "stuff" can be destroyed—by us. This is a big shadow we are shining a light on.

How can we embrace this side of ourselves—this mirror image of our blessing? It has brought much comfort to say that the bad guys are the destroyers, not us, but the truth is, we are *all* destroyers and creators. Our power to both create and to detonate is enormous.

Now it is time to face the destroyer within ourselves and welcome it into our loving arms like a lost troublesome lamb that keeps wandering off. As love for ourselves grows within us, as we learn how to honor our paradoxes, we move deeper into grace. Our creative dance begins to fall in step with God's dance. So we may sing—Not my will but ours (mine and yours in harmony with God's) be done.

As we go further into our own shadows, we discover an unfathomable mystery. Because we are beings of light, our very entrance into our shadows brings light into our dark places.

I do not mean that by walking onto the scorched and scarred earth that once was a lush rain forest, that suddenly the damage will be undone and a new forest will appear. On the physical, material plane, time and space require trees to fall when chain sawed and bulldozed. But in the eternal realm of spirit, the light-loving energy of which the trees are made cannot be destroyed. The trees can be sawed and chipped and burned, but the spirit of the trees is eternal.

Just as there is no death of spirit, there is also no destruction—only creation, only life. But, oh how there appears to be! What happens in the outer, external, physical world is a parable for what happens in our own interior worlds. What happens in the entire cosmic realm happens within each of us. In the cosmic realm, we, the trees, the animals, fish, birds, flowers, mountains, all beings are connected, and all are made out of light and out of love. When any of us incarnate, that is, when we take on a physical form, we can have a material effect on each other's forms. A rock can fall and cut your skin; a crocodile can eat a bird; a volcano can erupt and cover a town in lava; an oil company can kill thousands of fish and birds with oil spills and pollution; a terrorist can set off a bomb killing and maiming many people.

No one would argue that, in the physical, visible realm, we can alter the physical forms of others in destructive ways. And, of course, we can harm our own bodies as well. There are predators and wars within us mirroring the predators and wars around us.

There are huge predators now roaming the rain forest, destroying vast sanctuaries of trees, animals, and indigenous people. These predators are the mega-companies which look at the forests as disposable commodities, treasure chests which once emptied, can be tossed aside as trash. The displaced people and vanished ecosystems have not been a concern to these companies, because they have not understood that the people and animals and plants are all sacred. They do not yet understand that the inhabitants of the rain forest are their brothers and sisters and that, what the companies do to the rain forest, they do to themselves.

There are predators roaming within our own psyches, as well. They threaten our ego systems with low self-esteem. These predators can wreak havoc with the choices we make, piling guilt and shame upon us as we try to make our way through life. Haven't we all in some small ways, ravaged our own interior rain forests by not paying full attention to the needs of ourselves as whole body-mind-spirit beings? Drug addiction, alcoholism, and anorexia are examples of self-ravaging. Even something as seemingly insignificant as throwing a styrofoam cup into a lake is a form of self-destruction as it ignores the sacred context within which we live and our interconnectedness with the life around us.

In this way, our internal affairs mirror the affairs of the world. As within, so without. That is why, as we heal ourselves, that is, as we whole ourselves—by embracing all that we are, including our paradoxes, our shadows, and our brightnesses—we also help to heal all creation. Likewise, when giant companies and governments learn to face their critics and acknowledge their trailing shadows of destruction, then they will be better positioned, like us, to align themselves with Divine Creativity. Any entity, no matter how small or large, which is able to embrace its contradictory wholeness and find its grace in this realm, will find itself a conduit of free-flowing innovations and ideas that will honor our inner and interconnectedness. At such a higher level of consciousness, we no longer operate out of a doctrine of 'every man for himself', but rather a whispered faith that every being is sacred and connected.

As we journey on toward higher consciousness in the midst of continuing violence, let us find some comfort in knowing that on the unchanging, spiritual plane, the spirits of all the ravaged trees; all the lost tribes; all the murdered and abandoned children; all the extinct animals and plants; all the animals and people who have been tortured and imprisoned, live on. Though their physical bodies are no longer with us, their spirits continue to shed love upon the earth. For they, like us, are made of love. At the level of spirit and high consciousness, they hold no animosity or desire for revenge. They understand that everything on earth whether it results in destruction or creation or a mixture of both is a lesson in love.

THE CHAKRA CONNECTION:
FIFTH BLESSING—CREATIVITY
FIFTH CHAKRA—EXPRESSION

> *There lives a creative being inside*
> *all of us, and we must get out of its*
> *way, for it will give us no peace unless we do.*
> —M.C. Richards

May the blessing of creativity flow through you at the place in you where your fifth chakra vibrates. The fifth chakra is generally believed to be located at the throat. This area involves the thyroid gland, the esophagus, mouth, and neck.

This is, of course, our avenue of expressing ourselves verbally to others. Through our throat chakra can come lies and lullabies, curses and blessings, screams and songs. The issues we deal with at the throat chakra level are choices: what to create, what to say, what to do. Located, as it is, between heart and head, we often feel tongue-tied or choked up when there is a disparity between our emotions and our logic. When this happens, our body is trying to talk to us.

The breath of God moves through this passageway many times each minute. Therefore, there is great wisdom at the fifth chakra. Sit quietly a few moments and listen to your breathing. Listen to it as it fills your nostrils and swooshes like wind in a tunnel into your lungs. What is it you are breathing? It is so much more than air. Ahh. It is life essence. Without that simple physiological miracle, our bodies would perish. What a fantastic metaphor is breathing. It is the Divine penetrating our bodies with Life and we, *our higher selves—in total harmony with God*, agreeing to receive Life into the body. In this way, through harmonizing our will for life with God's will for life, we co-create a body with God. It is with each breath that our will is one with that of our Beloved Creator.

Often, at night, when my children were small, I would sit beside them as they slept and just listen to their soft, rhythmic breathing. It was, to me, the sweetest sound on earth, and it always made me cry. The sound of angels singing could not have been more beautiful, because to me it meant they were here on earth with me sharing this amazing adventure. Imagine, then, how the Divine Mother-Father, who loves you infinitely, must weep with joy at the mere sound of your sighs.

> *If I can get out of the way, if I can*
> *be pure enough, if I can be selfless*
> *enough, and if I can be generous*
> *and loving and caring enough to*
> *abandon what I have and my own*
> *preconceived, silly notions of what*
> *I think I am—and become truly who*
> *in fact I am, which is really just*
> *another child of God—then the*
> *music can really use me, and therein*
> *lies my fulfillment. That's when the*
> *music starts to happen.*
> —John McLaughlin, 20th century musician

EXPERIENCING THE CREATIVITY BLESSING

1. Make two lists. One will be a list of three things that have happened in your past that have brought you bliss—true high points in your life when you felt in synch with the universe. The other will be a list of three times when you felt extremely angry about something and everything felt out of synch. These are lights and shadows from your past. They both carry valuable information for you. Review your lists. What do they tell you about your inner world of light and shadow? How do those angry times relate to the blissful times? Both are times

of passion; both hold the treasure of self-knowledge and aware-ness. From the point of view of your higher self, embrace your entire, richly passionate self. As you embrace that holy oneness, what key words come immediately to mind as very unique aspects of you? Write them down.

2. List five or more things in your life that are fun to you, that draw you, that you catch yourself dreaming about, that you know would bring you joy. Some of these may be the same as in your bliss list in #1. These are significant clues to the future you can create for yourself. No matter how busy you are at this time in your life with day to day responsibilities, indulge yourself. Give these dreams room to grow in your heart. Open yourself to the possibility of pursuing some or all of them, re-membering all the while, *the power of creativity is flowing through you right now and all the time.*

3. If you are trying to decide whether or not to pursue a certain dream, this can be a helpful exercise: Close your eyes and breathe deeply and slowly. Now imagine you are your higher self observing your earth self achieving a certain goal. See your earth self in a scene in which your goal is achieved. See all the details about it. Fill your senses with any aspects of it such as smells or sounds. Fill in the scene, perhaps, with other people. They could be customers or admirers or family. Feel all the feelings about it. Does it feel good? Does it feel worth the effort it would take to achieve it? It it doesn't feel quite right, it's probably not where you want to go, and your intuition knows that. So just let it float away from your awareness. If, on the other hand, it feels right and in harmony with your higher self, then breathe life into it. Bless it. Believe it. Take action.

A PRAYER

Divine Creator of all Holy Creation
Thank You for helping us to receive and fully understand our blessing of creativity. Thank You for helping us to comprehend that, not only we human beings, but 'all our relations'—plants, stones, trees, everyone— are blessed in this way.

How generously, how graciously You guide us to know and love who we really are so that we may express the best of who we really are, so that we may give and share love in our own unique way.

We feel You reaching forth to help us to sense, intuit, love, and breathe Your Wise Will, so that we may be co-creators with You. Oh, Grand and Loving Sculptor of the Universe, it is You we thank for all of this help and for breathing Life and Love into our souls and bodies. And it is You who tries to show us every day that we ourselves are composers with You of this sweet symphony of Life.

It is with You that we stand at the point of creation where spirit is birthed into matter, on the precipice where Heaven leaps fearlessly into Earth. We feel the rush of energy as You move through each of us, proclaiming—"Behold, Love is visible in this My child—Look—Look—My Love is here and everywhere!"
Om Amen Ho

6th

BLESSING

YOU ARE PERFECT

When you feel lost, alone, different, or full of faults, remember—you are perfect to Me right now just as you are. I see only Exquisite Beauty, Elegance, Grace, and Ecstasy in you, Beloved. If the world seems to judge you or the path you have taken, remember there is no "wrong" path home to Me. You are already here in My arms this very day.

The Blessing of Perfection

We find that life is a miracle, the universe is a miracle, and we too are a miracle.

—Thich Nhat Hanh, 20th century Vietnamese spiritual teacher

You are here. *And you are beautiful beyond reason, beyond logic.* Gaze, as your lover would, into your own eyes. Use a mirror or close your eyes and imagine you—as your soul self—looking lovingly into your own eyes. I want you to see the ocean of you; the volcanic light of heaven of you; the breathing, blazing dragon of you; the snorting, pawing giant bull of you; the tiny, white feather of you, too light to fall; the snowflake of you no one has ever seen before.

Look—see the sacred burning fire in your eyes. See the breath of Almighty Life flaring your nostrils and announcing to the world—I am here!!

This is your perfection. This is the whole and holy you that lives eternally, beyond duality, outside of good and evil. This is the you that came to earth to play and experiment with the Tree of the Knowledge of Good and Evil, with matter, with longings and lust, with life and death, with time and space.

This is the you that knows your perfection intimately and whispers to you in times of trouble—"Self, this heartache will pass, but you, *you who are pure joy*, will go on forever."

A woman named Simone Weil was engaged in day to day living and not actively pursuing God, but one day she experienced Christ himself coming to her and taking "possession" of her. Thereafter, she became an avid student of the Bible, the Bhagavad-Gita, and other spiritual literature, and she often experienced mystical states of awareness herself. In those states, she journeyed to a realm beyond space and time, a realm where there was no judgment, "neither perspective, nor point of view."

St. Joseph of Cupertino of the 17th century showed us what can happen to our bodies when we let go of duality and immerse ourselves in ecstasy. Very often St. Joseph would simply be so full of joy that he could not stay on the ground and would literally levitate or float up to the ceiling of the monastery or out in the open air. Paramahansa Yogananda wrote about this and noted that Joseph's "monastery brothers could not permit him to serve at the common table, lest he ascend to the ceiling with the crockery."

St. Teresa of Avila was also given to levitation without any conscious effort or intention, so full of joy was she. Her body was buried near a Spanish church. Visitors to the church have seen miracles there and often notice the fragrance of flowers at the burial site.

Would these saints tell us we're not levitating or performing miracles because we're bad and they are good, or that they are perfect and we are imperfect? No. Instead, I think they would tell us we're not levitating because we're not in ecstasy, and we're not in ecstasy only because we've forgotten our perfection, and because we have forgotten that God is wildly and fiercely in love with each one of us.

> *The source of the soul is perfect, and*
> *so is its goal; therefore, ...the soul has*
> *the spark of perfection.*
> —Pir-O-Murshid Inayat Khan, 20th century Sufi

> *As soon as we arrived, they brought*
> *a man full of worms. They had*
> *picked him up in a sewer. For three*
> *hours I have been touching the body*
> *of Christ. I know it was He.*
> —A nun telling Mother Teresa about her day
> tending the sick and dying, 20th century, India

YOU ARE ENFOLDED WITH PERFECTION

> *Once grasp the great form without*
> *form, and you roam where you will*
> *with no evil to fear, calm, peaceful,*
> *at ease.*
> —Lao Tzu, 600 B.C. Chinese philosopher and founder of
> Taoism

Quantum physicists are telling us that our bodies are just a tiny part of who we are. Our physical senses tell us only a fragment of all that is going on. We are capable of exploring beyond our five senses and our physical bodies and going to realms of infinite wisdom and love. We are non-local beings these physicists are saying. We live and move and vibrate both within and outside the apparent confines of our skin. We are so big, in fact, we can't be measured, so big that bigness doesn't even have a meaning.

We have lived in fear of punishment for being sinners long enough. The truth is rising like a mist on a mountain lake. We can all see it if we look. We are one with the levitating saints and the miracle workers. We are all birthed from the same Perfection. The same Holy Omnipresence that is within the mystics is also within us. What we are learning is that performing good deeds is not a means to gain heaven and avoid hell. Rather it is a consequence, a joyous result of remembering our own Divine Perfection.

Scientists, saints, and mystics show us and tell us that we all have the capacity to experience within ourselves the ecstasy of oneness, the ravishing ardor of non-dualism. We ourselves, our spirits, are one with All-That-Lives. When we are fully conscious in our oneness, we are in love with All, including ourselves, completely incapable of seeing imperfection anywhere.

Within the province of time and space, our bodies and brains separate and categorize and judge. And all the while our spirits smile and wait for the rest of us to catch up and see the whole, undivided, unseparated Awesome Unum. From the many—one.

W.C. Ellerbroek, a physician, has documented 57 cases of miracle cures of cancer. These are cases of people who should have died from cancer and didn't. He found a common factor among these 57 to which he attributes their miracle cures. Each one, believing they had only a short time left to live, gave up their feelings of anger and depression (that is, judgments that things were bad). They decided that, in the time left, they would spend their days loving and caring and not spend energy on resentment. And then, to their surprise, they didn't die. The news of their impending departure was the spark they needed to ignite their awareness of what is true and permanent. Judgment and resentment seem meaningless and useless when remembrance of our unity and perfection is fully awakened.

Physicist David Bohm's Implicate Order theory, which was published in 1980, proposes that there is no disorder. Classical science has maintained that all things can be classified. They are either ordered like the bodies of living creatures or disordered and random like a building that has been demolished. Bohm theorized that things we perceive to be random or disordered actually have an implicate or intrinsic order that we cannot, at the moment, see.

For example, the interference patterns on a piece of holographic film appear to be random, but because there is order hidden or enfolded in the patterns, an image can be projected that we can recognize and thus consider ordered.

Bohm joined the company of mystics when he further proposed that what we see and touch in the space-time realm of our earth lives is like a holographic image. Beyond the confines of the visible, there is an implicate reality within which every thing is enfolded. What we see here and now is unfolded into the visible. It is implicate, invisible stuff which has become what he calls explicate or visible stuff.

This implicate order is our state of perfection. As spirits, we are enfolded with perfect order. We unfold over and over into the explicate order, moving and dancing with the Uni-verse, the One Verse that births all songs. Out of the Implicate Womb of music come explicate love songs and gangster music and back to the womb they return, still ordered, still perfect.

> *In motion they separate, in stillness they fuse.*
> —Ancient principle of T'ai Chi

EXPECT LOVE, NOT JUDGMENT

> *One thing, all things, move among*
> *and intermingle without distinction.*
> *To live in this realization is to be*
> *without anxiety and non-perfection.*
> *To live in this faith is the road to*
> *non-duality, because the non-dual*
> *is one with the trusting mind.*
> —Sengstan, Third Zen Ancestor

> *Grandmother, she will cradle us*
> *again. She knows that we have*
> *been naughty, but instead of*
> *spanking us, she'll wipe away our*
> *tears and forgive us.*
> —Wallace Black Elk, 20th century, Native American Lakota shaman

Most people who have lived through a near death experience (often called NDE's) are amazed to find that there is no judgment in the realm of the afterlife. The beings of light that greet them offer them love, acceptance, and wisdom, but no condemnation, no judgment. It is as if, Bohmianly speaking, we leave our implicate order and unfold ourselves out into the explicate order of earth life for a time. We journey about learning all we can of love from every possible angle and, then, fold back into our implicate, perfect, spirit selves once again. We are welcomed back as the perfect beings of love that we truly are.

The idea of going beyond duality and judgment is very much related to the concept of oneness and belonging which is our second blessing. We live in an unbroken, seamless whole. A physician named Larry Dossey believes that healing can emerge within us when we stop thinking dualistically in terms of sickness versus health and instead see sickness and health as linked together in a larger whole.

As an example, he describes an experiment with epileptic children. These children were videotaped as they interacted with their families. Many seizures were recorded during these sessions. When the children watched the tapes, they were able to see their seizures and how the seizures related to the bigger picture of their lives in general and their relationships. After working in this way, the children significantly reduced the number of seizures they experienced. By folding the seizures into the larger pattern of their lives, what seemed to be chaotic, external, and destructive, was embraced and given meaning and purpose.

In our own encircling of all that we are and in our own compassionate gazing at all that we are, we get glimpses— starbursts and flashes—of our true perfection. And some of the weight of our pain begins to lift.

YOU ARE EXACTLY WHERE YOU NEED TO BE

You are doing exactly what you need to be doing this moment and this day. You are where you need to be and where you can be. You are learning how to love as well and as fast as you can. The Great Holy One shepherds us all into safe places, and there will be no lost sheep.

Many wars have been fought and many people killed, because certain groups of people thought they knew there was only one way to God, one true religion, or one true government. Ralph Bennett reports that today nearly 200 million Christians in China, Pakistan, Bangladesh, and other countries are being persecuted, tortured, enslaved, and killed, simply because they are Christians and refuse to renounce their faith. In the last decade, half a million Christians in Sudan have been killed. Tibetan Buddhists, who are still in Tibet, are in grave danger from the Chinese government. Their spiritual leader, the Dalai Lama is living in exile, having escaped some years ago. Not that many centuries ago, Christians brutally persecuted non-Christians during the Crusades.

In less murderous ways, some fundamentalist Christians wage televised war, labeling such ancient religions as Hinduism, Buddhism, and other "non-Christian" ideologies, as satanic and something to be feared. In 1997, the Southern Baptist Convention instituted a boycott of all Disney related products, programs, and parks, because Disney's business policies were favorable to gay men and women. This policy ignores the discovery made by millions of God's mystics, saints, and shamans that *we are all, each and every person, animal, plant, and pebble—sacred, important, and beautiful.* We are not judged good or bad by God. We are perfectly loved.

As a result, none of us will be lost: not the fundamentalist Christians, gays, or Disney; not the Buddhists, Hindus, or Native Americans; not Hitler or the Neo-Nazis; not the new agers. Neither the oppressors or the oppressed will be lost, for we are all offspring of the Loving Shepherd who cares for each one of us.

We are all part of each other, mirroring back and forth different facets of humanity that we must learn about in order to finally see our spiritual perfection. We are all trying on different hats and different crowns; all walking different paths, scaling different mountains. We are all journeying along different spokes, but we are going toward the same hub. It is the hub of conscious joy and unity. As long as we are way back on our spoke, we cannot see the rest of the wheel. We cannot see that we are all on that same wheel. But as we get closer to the hub, as we are now beginning to do in ever larger numbers, the consciousness begins to dawn, and dawn brings light. And in the light we see, *we are all one, all divine, all perfect and beautiful and linked by Love.* Not one of us, no matter what we believe or don't believe, not one of us can ever be lost to this Great Gentle All-Forgiving Love.

You are the way and the wayfarers,
and when one of you falls down he
falls for those behind him, a caution
against the stumbling stone. Ay, and
he falls for those ahead of him, who
though faster and surer of foot, yet
removed not the stumbling stone.
—Kahlil Gibran

IN SPIRIT YOU WILL FIND YOUR PERFECTION

The Magical Child emerges when the
wounded inner child is embraced
and nourished. Our true self is
eternal and enduring. It persists
throughout all change. It survives
as our Magical Child.
—John Bradshaw, 20th century American counselor and
seminar leader

It is much easier to understand and accept that we are perfect as we are when we identify with our spirit, when we look at
our bodies from our spirit's point of view. Our spirit does not
suffer. It sees everything that we do and everything that happens on earth as an opportunity to learn more about love and
compassion. Like God, it forms no judgements about what is
good and what is bad. Like God, our spirit calls us to be in the
spirit, rather than in the suffering. The human mind and body,
on the other hand, can get locked in the duality of matter: right
and left, good and bad, beautiful and ugly, shallow and deep,
dark and light.

These discernments are often necessary for simple physical
survival. For example, we must avoid menacing looking people
in dark alleys at night. However, these polarities, when taken
too much to heart, can cause us to rebuke ourselves and others
for not being more educated, richer, better dressed, more so-
ciable, more articulate, etc. Our inner critic has an endless list

and taunts us ever onward to the elusive goal of perfection. But because the list is endless, we finally run out of time and energy, and that perfection that we sought in ourselves and our environment is never reached.

How then can I say, *you are perfect?* It is because, in the eyes of God, you are indeed. Have you ever had a love unrequited? One that you had to let go while still the glow of new romance was fresh as dew? The sweet, unbearable longing so intensifies at the final parting that one wonders if there will ever be relief.

I know this—that the farther you stray from the Fingertips of the Great Cosmic Lover, the greater and more ignited is the All Consuming Passion to be with you again. And that Great Love will never rest until you, in all your Divine Perfection, are home in the Loving Arms once more.

> *Between God and the soul, there is not between.*
> —Julian of Norwich, 15th century English mystic

THE GRAND PARADOX: PERFECTION'S INTIMATE DANCE WITH DUALITY

> *Life is not a problem to be solved.*
> *It is a mystery to be lived.*
> —Soren Kierkegaard, 19th century Danish philosopher

> *There are only two ways to live*
> *your life. One is as though nothing*
> *is a miracle. The other is as though*
> *everything is a miracle.*
> —Albert Einstein, 20th century American scientist

The opposite of our sixth blessing of perfection, that is paradoxically contained within it, is duality and imperfection. Imperfection has its roots in duality. It springs up from our endless duels over what is right and what is wrong; what is good and what is evil. Our own frustrating drive for perfection in ourselves is never satisfied or finished because we are looking at ourselves through the lenses of duality, judging ourselves according to the insatiable, constantly changing system of rights and wrongs.

We live, all at once, on many levels. While it may seem to be a contradiction to say we are both perfect and imperfect, it is not. It is at the level of spirit that we find our perfection, and it is at the physical level of body and mind that we find ourselves immersed in the tabloid world of good and bad. And we are all of these—body, mind, and spirit.

It appears to be our task to learn to look at good and evil without judgment; then, to hold the tension created by that restraint of judgment. It is somewhere in the holding and the waiting that we eventually discover the unity that plays hide and seek with us behind duality.

I have a number of clients and friends who claim that life threatening illnesses, though initially perceived to be an evil enemy of the body, turned out to be a most valued teacher. Out of their dark suffering with cancer and other illnesses, they emerged with a deeper appreciation for life, loved ones, and themselves than they had ever known. In the Bible, when Jacob wrestled with the angel, he announced, "I will not let you go until you bless me." In that same manner, these people wrestled with illness and let it go only after it blessed them.

As Pir Vilayat Khan puts it: "When we come across a once-devastated person who has emerged from the ordeal transfigured, cleansed, and bubbling with joy, suddenly suffering reveals its true significance."

> *Good and evil is the challenging*
> *riddle which life places sphinxlike*
> *before every intelligence....Here and*
> *there , a towering lonely figure*
> *never cries defeat. From the maya*
> *(cosmic illusion) of duality he plucks*
> *the cleaveless truth of unity.*
> —A wandering sadhu in 20th century India, quoted by
> Paramahansa Yogananda

HATRED MAKES LOVE MORE PRECIOUS

> *If we allow ourselves to believe in*
> *it [perfection] and all that flows*
> *from it, we then open ourselves to*
> *the constant experience of our*
> *natural state which is joyfulness.*
> *This is the way we express our per-*
> *fection, and thus our gratitude for*
> *the incredible gifts that are given*
> *to us.*
> —Arnold Patent, 20th century American writer

> *I will speak ill of no man...and speak*
> *all the good I know of everybody.*
> —Benjamin Franklin, 18th century American
> statesman and writer

We know from much psychosomatic research now that dishonesty with ourselves and others weakens the immune system. Holding onto bitterness and resentment toward ourselves and others can create tumors and other unwanted growths. Self-hatred can cause the body to turn against itself leading to depression, fatigue, addictions, accidents, even suicide.

Perhaps, in some sense, our bodies are the angels we wrestle with. Perhaps, it is our bodies that push and shove us with pains and ailments and get our attention with broken bones and bleeding wounds. Perhaps, our bodies are the canaries in the mines of our spiritual treasure. While we eagerly seek spiritual peace and love, our canaries tell us that we're running out of oxygen or that things are getting pretty toxic.

In that way, through physical pain and illness, our bodies draw us back to the work of embracing and loving ourselves in our totality. This is important, because, as we grow in remembrance of who we are, we must bring our whole selves along or amnesia will overtake us once again. Toxic emotions, such as hate and resentment, work in the same way. They are not intrinsically bad. They come to us like dark angels with great wisdom for our souls.

In the same way that physical pain alerts us to our need to turn back and gather in the lost sheep of ourselves, so too does emotional pain. Hatred is the primary emotion of dual or polarized thinking, and fear is its foundation. Hatred and fear allow us to see the hated other as worse than and different from ourselves. Hatred justifies "moral wars," yet hatred is the canary that gasps the loudest. Wayne Dyer, well known author and speaker, tells us that if we hate our neighbors and behave in harmful ways toward them, that tells us how much we hate ourselves and that we are going to behave in harmful ways toward ourselves. Wallace Black Elk, a Lakota shaman, was committed to a mental hospital and treated badly there. He was committed there for practicing his faith. A spirit came to comfort and help him, because Wallace had continued to love the people who committed him and treated him badly. The spirit told Wallace to keep loving them no matter what they did to him.

> *Now, the peculiar predicament is that when you see any kind of injustice in the world, if you are attached to anger about it, or are attached to it being any other way, you are at one level perpetuating the polarization even as you are working to end it.*
> —Ram Dass, 20th century American writer and spiritual teacher

DANGER GIVES US VISION

Life is very dangerous, and it's also very safe. That's how it is maybe all the time, both dangerous and safe. That's how a prisoner in a concentration camp who is being tortured daily can come to the conclusion that she is absolutely safe in the arms of the Great Protector and loved beyond all reason.

That's how we might be drawn helplessly into the safe nest of our lover's arms while simultaneously fearing the sudden unraveling of that nest.

Because we know there is much to fear; and yet there are quiet pools of nurturing love all along the paths of our lives.

Would we know we were safe if we had never experienced danger? Our souls seek out danger. As human beings we are restless. We long for the hero's journey to prove ourselves, to etch ourselves against the hard rock of reality, to prove to ourselves that we exist—we're here! Does anybody notice me?

Life holds out its hand to us, and in it lies the sweet, holy rush of danger to help define us; and in it also lies the breezy hush of safety in the sacred arms of Love to help us be strong. Our higher selves, our wondrous souls push our bodies and personalities gently forward like parents urging toddlers forward on wobbly little legs. Out into the world of possibilities we venture. Without trust in the safety of Love, we hesitate. Without the tangled, treacherous path ahead, we wither.

Perhaps, we seek out more and more intense forms of danger or trouble as we seek new visions. The Native American vision quest is an example of consciously bringing danger into one's life in order to achieve a new sense of purpose. On a vision quest, one ventures into the wilderness with few provisions and fasts alone for a number of days. The body senses a crisis, and the ensuing alertness and other biochemical changes that take place help to open the mind to greater possibilities for the soul.

Each one of us is on our own vision quest, our own hero's journey. As we embrace both the safety and the danger, we allow ourselves access to our own personal, mysterious, and unique meaning and purpose.

> *...All the pain felt at the injustice*
> *and misery prevailing in the world,*
> *all the disappointment of shattered*
> *dreams and broken hopes, all the*

> *anguish of eternal partings from*
> *near and dear ones, and all the fear*
> *of ill health, decay, and death*
> *vanish like vapor at the rise of the*
> *inner sun, at the recognition of the*
> *inmost self, beyond thought, beyond*
> *doubt, beyond pain, beyond morta-*
> *lity which, once perceived, illumines*
> *the darkness of the mind as a flash*
> *of strong lightning cleaves the dark-*
> *ness of the nights...*
> —Gopi Krishna, 20th century Indian writer and spiritual
> teacher

> *Men, one by one, escape from*
> *creation's prison of duality as they*
> *awaken to consciousness of their*
> *inseverable divine unity with the Creator.*
> —Paramahansa Yogananda, 20th century

THE EMBRACE THAT LEADS TO UNITY

> *I am the frog swimming happily in*
> *the clear water of a pond, and I am*
> *also the grass-snake who, approach-*
> *ing in silence, feeds itself on the frog.*
> *I am the child in Uganda, all skin*
> *and bones, my legs as thin as bam-*
> *boo sticks, and I am the arms mer-*
> *chant, selling deadly weapons to*
> *Uganda.*
> —Thich Nhat Hanh, 20th century Vietnamese spiritual
> teacher

But what about the apparently truly evil among us—the Hitlers, the serial killers, the terrorists?

Out of the mud, the lovely lotus.
—Zen saying

The world outside of us is a mirror of the world inside us. As without—so within. The external world obeys the same laws of physics as our bodies do. One such law is known as the Principle of Complementarity. It states that the nature of light is paradoxical. It is both particle and wave. Physicist Niels Bohr offered up the suggestion that, in cases of paradox, consider that both sides are equally valid, neither one being better or more correct than the other. He hoped that we were ready to move into the understanding that "only wholeness leads to clarity." Only by embracing both sides of an issue can we reach the unity behind the paradox.

So, if the external world mirrors our internal worlds; and if clarity will come to us by embracing opposites, such as good and evil, then what?

Thomas Moore, author of *Soul Mates,* says that we sustain violence in our world when we refuse to admit that we hold it within our own hearts. Let us allow the possibility that there are serial killers within us, in our own psyches, strangling parts of ourselves; and children within us starving for lack of affection and nurturing. They show up in our dreams and in our waves of melancholy and in our mistakes in love and work and family.

In 1984, Michael Ross was arrested. He has confessed to raping and killing eight women and stalking and assaulting many others. He is now on death row in Connecticut and has expressed his wish to be executed so that his victims' families will not have to endure another trial. His compulsion to commit sexually sadistic crimes endured within him even after he was incarcerated and sentenced to death. Three years after he arrived on death row, Michael began taking injections of Depo-Provera and later, Depo-Lupron. The effect of the drugs was to reduce his body's production of testosterone to a prepubescent level of 20. The normal range of testosterone in adult males is 260 to 1,250.

As Michael's testosterone level dropped, his obsessions diminished with it. In his words, "I had my mind back—a clear mind free of malevolent thoughts and urges." He no longer was obsessed with violent thoughts and urges to do harm. His mind was clear. He felt free even though he was spending his life incarcerated on death row. For a while after this, Michael went through a period of blaming others for his actions, but finally he was able to begin looking within and accept responsibility for his own monstrous acts. This awakened in him a terrible agony, tormenting guilt and self-hatred and simultaneously and paradoxically "gave me back something I thought I had lost forever—my humanity."

Michael now lives with a deep yearning as he awaits his execution, a yearning for reconciliation with those he has harmed, both his victims and their families, as well as with God. He believes that murders such as he has committed can be prevented, not by turning our backs on the "evil" we perceive, but by facing and acknowledging it as something we can heal.

Like all of us, Michael Ross, is a spiritual being made of divine energy. Like us, he exists, because Love needed him into beingness. When he entered his physical body, he forgot his own holiness; he lost conscious contact with the Love he came to give. The consequences were tragic beyond measure. We want to eliminate the man with the madness. What has happened, however, is that by illuminating the madness, we have found the man.

In the same way, we find ourselves through illumination of all our shadows, rather than through elimination of them. By going through, rather than around, our tragedies and shortcomings, we eventually will view the light at the end of the tunnel from the inside.

It is this spiritual work which moves us closer to Gandhi and Martin Luther King who could see beyond blame, hatred, and pain to creative solutions. By going through our own psychic battles and embracing all that we are, we learn compassion for our inner enemies. And with that comes compassion for our outer enemies. And with that comes the perception of perfection in you and in all.

I have found that life persists in
the midst of destruction. Therefore
there must be a higher law than
that of destruction....Wherever there
are wars, wherever we are con-
fronted with an opponent, conquer by love.
—Mahatma Gandhi, 20th century Indian political and
spiritual leader

That only one who takes upon him-
self the evils of the world may be its
king. This is paradox.
—Lao Tzu, 600 B.C. Chinese philosopher and founder of
Taoism

COMPASSIONATE WARRIORS

We must recognize that the evil
deed of the enemy neighbor, the
thing that hurts, never quite ex-
presses all that he is. An element of
goodness may be found even in our
worst enemy.
—Martin Luther King, Jr., 20th century American
minister and civil rights leader

Does this mean we should stand by passively when someone is being attacked? Of course, the answer to that is no.
There is a time to be a warrior and to defend those in need. We
will all live those times, perhaps, long before we fully understand our oneness with the attacker. Yet there will be years following the attack during which our spirits can teach us
forgiveness and to find that "element of goodness" of which
Martin Luther King speaks.

A TV show you may have seen recounted the story of a
woman whose son was killed by a man who was trying to steal
her son's wallet. This woman visited her son's murderer in
prison many times for over a decade. Her family and friends

discouraged and even criticized her for doing so, but she persisted. She was determined to walk through the unbearable evil and find what she could of healing on the other side.

And what of the duality of sadness and joy? We want joy, not depression in our lives. Yet can any one of us escape melancholy completely, and is it really bad? Depression never lasts forever. We always come out of it somehow. It runs its course in time. As we gain life experience, we begin to see the natural progression. Sometimes, depression can get a really good hold on us, but thinking back, we see that something always breaks its death grip. Once we understand that it cannot hold us endlessly, we gain more courage to look it in the face and find out what it has come to teach us. With courage, we can dive deep into the flames, taste the sulfur, cry without caution. Faith stands to the side and waits, ready when we are to take us safely back to the ordinary day.

Let us linger for awhile in this depression. As the flames curl around our feet, we begin to understand that there is passion for life churning in the abyss of despair. It is a passion that cries out for meaning, for intensity, for vibrancy, for energy, for focus. It is a passion that knows there is more to life than we have been feeling. Somewhere in these hellish flames are coals that we can take back with us to home's hearth. It is in this courageous surrender to despair that we may more deeply integrate our psyches. And it is in that integration that we free our souls, a bit more each time, from duality.

As we free ourselves from inner duality, we assist all creatures and the cosmos itself to do the same. The inner despair and self-hatred of us all is projected onto the outer world in the form of racism, nuclear warfare, animal and human abuse, and environmental destruction. All of that is: us-in-our-oneness turning on our self in self-destruction. It follows that as we learn to love ourselves with all our dualities and contradictions and frustrations, we can likewise learn to accept and honor those dualities in others and recognize the sacredness of all creation.

When the mind is filled with God's
peace, all hatred ceases.

—Mahatma Gandhi, 20th century Indian spiritual leader

No peace lies in the future which is
not hidden in this present instant.
Take peace. The gloom of the world
is but a shadow; behind it, yet within
reach is joy. Take joy.

—Fra Giovanni, 15th century Italian painter and priest

INITIATION INTO TRUTH

The keys to compassion...lie in your
ability to embrace all experience
as part of the one without judgment...
Healing our sense of separation,
walking between the worlds (of
earth and heaven), is the path of
compassion.

—Greg Braden, 20th century American scientist

It is not through judgment that the
good can be reached, but through love and faith.

—Peace Pilgrim, 20th century American mystic

Our bodies, our relationships, and our spirits thrive on truth. We are being born and reborn over and over into clearer and brighter truth. Robert Bly and Marion Woodman, in their video series "Men and Women", tell us that a crisis is a signal to us that our next initiation into truth is trying to happen. Some crises will repeat themselves over and over until we finally see the pattern and allow the initiation to happen.

There are tribal initiations in which one's body is cut and scarred, vision quests of fasting and solitude, and mythic initiations in which the hero must slay the dragon or outwit the witch. Our own initiations are the same, just as dark and scary and lonely. They come to us to reveal to us our own perfection and the holiness of all life.

Initiation is not so much a transformative process as it is a medium through which our true "form" is revealed to us. Once we glimpse our perfection, it becomes clear that all the imperfections we have claimed as our own are simply markers for our births and rebirths. Without them we could not find our way to the site of the ceremony.

> *Nor in the bow that smiles in*
> *showers, but in the mud and scum*
> *of things, there alway, alway something sings.*
> —Ralph Waldo Emerson, 19th century American poet and essayist

> *All suffering prepares the soul for vision.*
> —Martin Buber, 20th century Jewish philosopher.

LOVING YOUR SHADOW

> *Our painful experiences that close*
> *around us like a tomb become the*
> *mold in which our wings are formed.*
> —Robert Wise, 20th century American writer

There has been a subtle advancement in our human consciousness in recent years. The idea of thinking only positive thoughts has been around for many years now. Anyone who has practiced positive thinking and affirmations knows the power that can be generated by doing that. Discarding or overriding negative thoughts and replacing them immediately with positive thoughts, such as thoughts of gratitude for what we have, demonstrates to us the power we, as spirits, have over the miraculous tool we call our brain. Through this practice, we can condition our minds, reprogram our thoughts, and thus increase the joy in our lives.

Now, as we evolve in the understanding of how our psyches work, we are seeing that, while the methods of positive thinking and affirmations are powerful tools, our negative thoughts have value as well. We now understand that those previously unwanted thoughts are soulful cries from within that may need attention and love. They represent our shadow, help define our individualty, and simply must be embraced in order for us to find our wholeness.

By cutting away unwanted thoughts as if they were enemies of the self, we may amputate parts of ourselves and leave ourselves less than whole. This is the evolutionary revelation that everything about us is blessed, even that which appears not to be. It is by looking deeply into the eyes of our shadow selves, respecting the wisdom we find there, and integrating the shadow into our sacred selves, that we find the authentic inner peace we seek. Once such work is in progress, positive thinking becomes much easier and more natural. It is in this way that we can find the nonjudgmental, unconditional love of self which leads to bliss, to inspired acts, and to a reverence for all life.

> *But what I'd seen that morning was*
> *loss and gain, not as opposites, but*
> *as the seamless fabric of life itself.*
> *Father, help me to see the dark*
> *threads too as part of your design.*
> —Elizabeth Sherrill, 20th century American writer

OUT OF MISERY—JOY

> *Forgiveness is the fragrance the*
> *violet sheds on the heel that has crushed it.*
> —Mark Twain, 19th century American author
> and humorist

> *To know all is to forgive all.*
> —Dale Carnegie, 20th century American writer

John Bradshaw, author of *Creating Love,* describes a process whereby many of us, as children, polarized our parents. We separated them into the good parent when they were treating us the way we wanted, and the bad parent when they weren't. So Mom and Dad were not whole, synthesized people in our childish perceptions. Rather they were each two separate entities—a bad mom, and a good mom, a bad dad, and a good dad.

As we learn to respectfully integrate our own mistakes and unpleasant traits into our personal sacred self, we find it comes much easier to do that for our parents and others. They are neither superman nor Satan. They are instead both annoying and delightful, distant and close, hateful and adorable.

We can simultaneously dislike our husbands or wives and love them as well if we will allow that. It is that love that tells us God is here right now, and it is that dislike that makes us long to see Divinity. I submit to you that every obnoxious and awful act against you, whether by lovers or strangers, is another knot in the rope that leads you deeper within you to Creator and to Love.

In a Japanese prison camp in Sumatra in 1943, women and children were dying from abuse, malnutrition, and disease. In the midst of the terrible suffering two women, Norah Chambers and Margaret Dryburgh, conceived a most amazing plan. Together they painstakingly wrote down the notes to some of the world's greatest music from memory and invented a way to teach a chorus of women to sound the notes as if they were instruments in an orchestra. As one woman wrote: "When I sang, I forgot I was in the camp. I felt free." This music, now memorialized in the 1997 movie "Paradise" and sung all over the world by women's choirs is a reminder to us all that "out of such an ugly place came music that still brings joy and solace throughout the world."

Helen Colijn, one of the survivors of the prison camp and author of *Song of Survival,* made that statement. She also shares with us the words of her father to her mother before he was killed at the camp, "Whatever happens, don't feel bitter. Bitterness will destroy you."

*Nondualism integrates the psyche
in such a way that energy once used
to repress or project now becomes
available for more creative activity.*
—Michael Zimmerman, 20th century writer

FINDING YOUR FEARLESS PERFECTION

*No matter how destructive, cruel,
and bad it may be, every aspect of
energy and consciousness is in its
original essence both beautiful and positive.*
—Eva Pierrakos, 20th century spiritual teacher

*...In the realm of the sacred, what
seems incomplete or unattainable
may be abundance after all.*
—Kathleen Norris, 20th century American writer

Every unpleasant or miserable situation is a helper, a guide. Look at the chaos and know there is order yet enfolded within it. Breathe, be still, penetrate the chaos quietly—what do you see? Where do you tingle? What powers are awakening within you?

Sri Gyanamata of the Self Realization Fellowship tells this little story from a book she once read, about a master who sometimes threw stones at his disciples. Those disciples who were full of reverence and desire for God treasured the stones and the stones turned to gold.

The world watches democracies at work. What is democracy but an embracing of opposites? The ideal democracy asks to hear all points of view, no matter how demanding or crazy or scattered, and then tries to find a synthesis that honors all. In similar fashion, we can establish democracies within us, honoring all our sub-personalities and our inner warring factions, giving them all a voice, respecting the wisdom of each. Ultimately we leave the final decision and veto power in the hands of our *seven-times-blessed higher self* whose goal is our eternal joy and our unity with God-In-All.

God's angels sing to us continually. Barely audible have they been above the rhythmic litany of our sins. But listen. The songs are growing louder now—songs of unity and songs of love. We are entering a new time, leaving our duality and polarized, either-or thinking behind.

Let us see the reflection of our Divine essence everywhere. We are witnessing a *soular warming*, a melting of the poles, a polar shift of quite cosmic proportions.

For too long we have waged our internal wars, demanding perfection of ourselves. Why have we done this? Because of fear. We fear that if we are not perfect, we will not be loved. The greatest paradox of all may be this: *that it is in loving our whole selves with all our temporary imperfections, that we find our true and permanent perfection.* It works that way, because the more we love ourselves, the less we have to fear. The more we become acquainted with our true divine nature, the less we fear abandonment and loss. And the less fear we feel, the more room there is within us for the Perfect Love that we truly are to show itself to us and through us.

> *What the caterpillar calls the end*
> *of the world, the master calls a butterfly.*
> —Richard Bach, 20th century American writer

> *Oh, Fletch,...you don't love the hatred*
> *and evil, of course. You have to*
> *practice and see the real gull, the*
> *good in every one of them, and to*
> *help them see it in themselves. That's*
> *what I mean by love. It's fun when*
> *you get the knack of it.*
> —Richard Bach, quoting Jonathan Livingston Seagull

THE CHAKRA CONNECTION:
SIXTH BLESSING—PERFECTION
SIXTH CHAKRA—WISDOM

May the blessing of perfection flow through you at the place in you where your sixth chakra vibrates and spirals. The sixth chakra is usually described as located at the center of the forehead. It is sometimes called the brow chakra and often referred to as the third eye or spiritual eye.

The brain and pituitary gland are energetically connected to the sixth chakra. It is by developing our second sight, our interior, intuitive wisdom, that we come to recognize our perfection as spiritual beings. It is through the unblocking and fine tuning of this chakra that we learn to observe ourselves objectively and embrace our whole selves: our darkness and light, our good and bad, our heavenliness and our earthiness. As we uncover and unblock our wisdom, we get flashes—like lightning momentarily lighting up the night sky—flashes of us immersed in our unity, glimpses of us in our perfection.

Remember those secret code games in which we placed a piece of red cellophane over a set of letters? Without the red cellophane, the letters made no sense, but with it placed strategically over the letters, a message would be revealed. Please, more and more often, position the magic cellophane over the "I" you think you see and—squinting a bit—behold God's message standing out boldly. That message announces to all who can see that *you are perfect, divine, outrageously beautiful, and exquisitely loved.*

EXPERIENCING THE BLESSING

1. Sit quietly, breathe evenly and deeply. What is the first thing that comes to your mind when I ask you this question: What bothers you the most about _____(this could be a spouse, parent, child, boss, etc.)? Write about that. Let yourself complain freely and spill out all your feelings about that. When you are finished, close your eyes and ask the higher self of the person who annoys you what it is they are trying to teach you

about yourself with this annoyance. Ask that person's higher self also how it can help you on your spiritual path.

Remember that enemies and annoyers mirror back to us where we have closed our hearts and tried to hide our own shadow. We try to hide our shadow because we fear it. Remember that love is more powerful than fear, always.

2. Again, get peaceful. Breathe deeply. Think of a decision that you need to make. It is a hard decision, because it seems to mean giving up one thing in order to get the other, and you want both. Picture yourself holding both these options—one in one hand and the other in the other hand. Admit to yourself that you want both of these things that seem incompatible. Feel the tension that is created by holding both options in your hands. Now, while you hold them, remember your seven blessings. Consider that, even if they don't seem true in this earthly, space-time realm, that in the realm of spirit, all the seven blessings are yours and are true.

Ask your higher self and your spiritual guides and the Great Lover of All to help you make your decision. Ask them to help you align your will with Divine Will. If an answer does not come immediately, *know that the answer will come to you at the perfect time.*

3. The following is a guided meditation. You may have someone read it to you; you might tape it; or you might read it to yourself as you meditate. Get comfortable and listen to your breathing for awhile with closed eyes. Now imagine yourself walking along a country road. You have on a light jacket and jeans and sandals. You have just recently begun experiencing long states of mystical awareness in which you are filled with ecstasy, and you are feeling such a state now. You feel as though your whole body is almost floating. It's like being in love, but even better.

Suddenly, dark clouds appear. The wind comes up. It begins to rain. Then, rain turns to snow. Your body is soaking wet and shivering. You notice that and think, "I need to get my body dry and warm."

Several cars drive by. You wave, but they don't stop. You think to yourself, "Ordinarily I would be scared and angry right now, but I can't shake this ecstasy." You feel love pouring through you to the drivers who passed you, and a strange sense that your body will be all right. As you walk on, the temperature drops below freezing. You come upon a farmhouse and rush to knock on the door. The occupant eyes you through the small window of the door and shakes his head. He refuses to help you. Incredibly, love rushes through you like a torrent to this man in the dark, unfriendly house, and you walk on—now, more ecstatic than ever, because of the love pouring through you. You are skipping and singing and dancing along the road in the bone chilling cold. How strange and wonderful to feel this joy in the midst of this dark storm.

Finally, you reach your home. You open the wooden door and rush into your cozy, warm living room. Strangely, your joyful ecstasy remains the same. You think, "In the past, I would have been miserable out in the storm and then suddenly thrilled and happy to be home and warm. But this time, I am filled with joy regardless of the circumstance. *I have found the river of joy within me; I have found the river of joy within me.*"

Now, bringing that sweetness along with you, come back to the present moment and open your eyes.

> *Spiritual work commences when one realizes he is in hell, and that he does not have to be.*
> —Jae Jah Noh

> *... be patient toward all that is un-solved in one's heart and try to love the questions themselves like locked rooms...Live the questions now. Perhaps you will then gradually, without noticing it, live along some distant day into the answer.*
> —Rainer Maria Rilke, 19th/20th century poet

A PRAYER

Oh, Holy Oneness, Father-Mother God

Thank You for teaching us how to uncover and truly see our own Divine Perfection with which we are so richly blessed. Thank you for helping us to glimpse the radiant perfection within all our brothers and sisters, and 'all our relations'.

Thank you for helping us in this, for it is one of our most difficult leaps of faith—to go beyond duality. We ate the fruit from the Tree of the Knowledge of Good and Evil. And while we struggled to learn to live in that way, you never left us. Always with unfailing attentiveness, you urged us up into the Tree of Life for a higher view—a view beyond duality, a view of the perfection and Divine Love in every being and in ourselves.

And, all the while, your Life Force pulses through us and through the Tree and through the beyond and keeps us whole and safe and loved.

Om Amen Ho

7th

BLESSING

YOU ARE DIVINE

There is nothing in Heaven or Earth that is not Sacred and filled with Me. I am in All-That-Is, and All-That-Is lives and breathes in Me. I am Life, and I am Love. Your spirit sees me looking lovingly back at you from every face, every drop of rain, every stone, and every gust of wind. When you look in the mirror, you see your face and Mine. There, in you, rejoices the Divine.

The Blessing of Divinity

*The soul is the immutable, unqualified image of
    God.*
—Sri Yukteswar, 19th and 20th century Indian yogi, quoted
by Paramahansa Yogananda

*Under the vast vault of blue lives
the divinity clothed in hide.*
—Ravidas, medieval Indian saint

Here is the ultimate blessing, the one that explains all the
others. Why are we innately immortal, dearly wanted, awesome
in our power, fiercely beloved, creative, and perfect? Because *we
are—each one of us—divine, holy, sacred offspring of Infinite Divinity.*

We are divine creatures, we are all beloved beings made of
light. We diligently seek ways to lighten up, to enlighten, to be
bright, to be a star, to shine; because, deep inside, we know our
dazzling origin.

Paramahansa Yogananda directly experienced the light of
himself one evening as he was meditating. In his autobiography, he recounts sitting on his bed in the lotus posture. As he
gazed upward, he saw a "transparent shaft" of light pouring
down upon him. He felt as if he were floating, as if he were
weightless. Then, he heard a voice saying: "This is a cosmic
motion picture mechanism. Shedding its beam on the white
screen of your bed sheets, it is producing the picture of your
body. Behold, your form is nothing but light."

Let us dive headfirst into our divinity. Perhaps, the ultimate
peace-in-us and peace-on-earth for which we long comes not
so much from sacrifice as from finally seeing the light streaming
from our own fingertips.

Knock, and He'll open the door.
Vanish, and He'll make you shine
like the sun.
Fall, and He'll raise you to the
Heavens.
Become nothing, and He'll turn you
into everything.
—Jalal ed-Din Rumi, 13th century Persian poet

YOUR BIRTHDAY IS A HOLY DAY

God poured the Divine being in equal
measure to all creatures, to each as
much as it can receive. This is a
good lesson for us that we should love
all creatures equally.
—Meister Eckhart, 13th century German theologian and
mystic

You created my inmost being; You
knit me together in my mother's
womb. I praise You because I am
fearfully and wonderfully made.
—David, 900 B.C. king of the ancient Hebrews, author of
many of the Psalms; Psalm 139:13-14

Let it be known, henceforth, that today, though it may not
be December 25, is Christmas Day. For on this day, in all lands
and seas across the earth, holy infants are being born. Miraculously conceived and given birth, the Cosmic Christ lives and
rejoices within each of them. Jesus and all the wise ones celebrate continually this endless Christmas Day.

Your own birthday is a holy day. You are a pure and faultless spirit. You have taken your form, your body, to help you
understand your true nature and to assist in filling the universe
with more love. You are love incarnate, capable of creating
more love wherever you go.

With the birth of each one of us, the sprouting of each seed, the opening of each egg and chrysalis, *the earth is filled with more love.* Each new physical body gives home to more love and gives expression to yet even more. Each one of your fingers can express life giving love in just one soft touch. Every sheltering wing, every fruit filled tree, every bedrock path gives love, and the more love that is given, the more, exponentially, love multiplies.

We are all Christs, Buddhas, Krishnas, shamans, and saints. It is not what we do so much that defines us thus, but what we are. But not knowing what we truly are can very much influence what we do. Acts of violence are committed by those who have forgotten that they are Love Incarnate.

May you know deep inside that you are holy, sacred, and beautiful. May you know that your birthday is a holy day, a Christmas day, and you are a gift to the universe.

> *One might say that the experience of pure intelligence is possible only for the Only Being, for God, but no one can stand outside of the Only Being, and, therefore, each and everyone is the Only Being.*
> —Pir-O-Murshid Inayat Khan, 20th century Sufi master

FALLING IN LOVE WITH LOVE

St. Theresa of Avila used to pray a simple prayer: "Domine, da mihi agua," which means, "Lord, give me the water." She was talking about the water of life that springs up eternally. It was the water that Jesus said would so satisfy us that we would never be thirsty again. Theresa's prayer was answered. During her many ecstasies, she was tasting that living water.

A twentieth century woman named Katharine Trevelyan described a period of ecstasy when she "felt as though an infinitely complex machine had in all its parts, between one moment and the next, clicked silently into gear and started to work with inexorable power. I was face to face at last."

When we do, finally, each one of us, drink the living water that has been forever flowing beside us; when we do finally, each one of us—you and I and everyone—do feel ourselves clicking silently into gear with the Divine; when we do finally take one furtive glance into the hall mirror, and, startled, stop and look again, and see God pouring through us—oh, Loving Creator, when that does happen, give us the strength to bear the bliss let loose within us.

In extremely high winds, it is advised that we minimize resistance by opening our windows or letting down our sails. As the full force gale of God's desire for us approaches, let us open our waiting hearts and fall helplessly in love with the Universal Love that Lives in All.

EVERYTHING IS LOVE, AND SO ARE YOU

> *Return again, return again,*
> *Return to the land of your soul.*
> *Return to who you are,*
> *Return to what you are,*
> *Be born and be reborn again.*
> —Jewish chant

Montague Ullman, a psychoanalyst, has proposed a perspective on dreams that differs from traditional scientific views. His ideas blend well with the use of dreams by indigenous people. Ullman offers the possibility that dreams may not be coming from a primitive part of the personality into the conscious dreaming mind. Instead, he suggests, they are messages from the implicate, non-manifest order to which we all have access. These dream messages, he suggests, are telling us in symbols how to know ourselves better and, thus, reach higher states of consciousness.

In that way the Great Spirit speaks to us in the parables of our dreams, gently prodding us to face the various 'good' and 'evil' parts of ourselves. In that way, we slowly get to know ourselves as whole and finally understand the ultimate, intimate truth of our own divinity. Once this divinity is recognized, we can then more fully express it and say: *"Everything is Love, and so am I!"*

Our bodies and personalities and brains are a bit like wonderful instruments that we are trying to learn how to play. We practice and practice, trying to express our spirits more and more soulfully through these instruments. It is easy to remember that we are the pianist when playing a piano. It is quite another task to remember we are the musician when trying to make heavenly music through the earthy instrument of our physical beings. We have a tendency instead to think we are only the instrument itself.

This is made even more confusing by the fact that our bodies, minds and personalities seem to have wills of their own. While our personalities may want to impress everyone with a slim, glamorous appearance, our bodies are demanding another piece of chocolate cake, and the mind is getting a headache from all the ruckus.

That is why there is great peace to be found in remembering that we are eternal spirits playing temporarily on earth in our bodies. We are the orchestra leaders. When one of our instruments breaks a string or a reed or plays poorly, when the music isn't quite what we want, we have the power to stop the music, take a deep breath, lift our batons and give it another try.

> *Every in-breath, you consume the universe; between the in-breath and the out-breath, you feed from God; then on the out-breath you feed humanity...you become the grace of God made manifest.*
>
> —Ram Dass, 20th century American spiritual teacher and writer

THE GRAND PARADOX: THE INTIMATE DANCE OF DIVINITY AND HUMANITY

> *[Regarding the fertilized human egg]*
> *The mere existence of that cell should*
> *be one of the greatest astonishments*
> *of the earth. People ought to be*
> *walking around all day, all through*
> *their waking hours, calling to each*
> *other in endless wonderment, talking*
> *of nothing except that cell.*
> —Lewis Thomas, 20th century author

The opposite of our seventh blessing of divinity which is paradoxically contained within it is our humanness. We think of divinity as being loving and wise, perfect and miraculous. Yet in our everyday lives on planet earth, we see ourselves and others making mistakes, being thoughtless, hurting each other. "We're only human," we protest. At times, we are frustrated with ourselves for falling short of perfection. At other times, we are frustrated with others who seem to be demanding perfection of us. In actuality, when we say, "we're only human," we are implying that we cannot be perfect, as if the word human were the very opposite of the word perfect.

If we saw a frog and knew nothing about biology, we might assume that's what a frog always looks like. Instead, we know that the frog goes through many stages from a divine implicate thought to an egg, a tadpole, a frog, a meal for a predator, then bones, then earth. Did the frog spirit ever leave the implicate order? No—the implicate order is replete and rich with the frog's sacred essence.

It is our enduring, eternal essence that is perfect and divine. It is our temporary physical presence to which we attach so much imperfection. But let us look a little more closely at this physical presence of ours.

Hans Yennie is a scientist who has filmed the amazing effect of music on sand and mugwort spores. He spreads the sand

and spores out on large trays and applies musical tones to the trays. The vibrations from the different tones cause the sand and spores to vibrate. Once they start vibrating, they begin to form designs. The higher the tone goes, the more complex the design becomes.

From a distance, the whole design is quite clear. However, if you look closely at the edges of the various lines in the design, you will see tiny grains of the medium moving in chaotic frenzy. Just looking at the edges, one would say there is no order here. However, if you back off again and look at the whole, it becomes clear that the grains are so *in-grained* with order that they very soon move out of the apparent chaos and click back into the design.

Does this sound like our lives? Sometimes our lives seem to be in hopeless chaos. Nothing seems to be going right. Nothing seems to be turning out as we planned it. But when we gain a little altitude, a little distance; when we look at our lives mindfully from the spirit's eye view—the rhythmic, vibrating design we see reveals the order that was there all along. It is up close, along the constantly changing edges, that it seems out of control. However, with a bit of distance and a good view, we can clearly see the Divine design.

With this model in mind, we can imagine a crew of subpersonalities within each of us: the frightened inner child, the demanding infant, the rebellious and confused adolescent, the imperfect mother or father, the inner critic, the self-hater, the romantic lover. There they are bumping into each other, vibrating to the powerful tones of belly laughs and mournful sobs.

Right there on the edge, caught in the midst of our bifurcated humanity, life can seem very loose and chaotic. But remember—we can fly. Our souls, our higher selves can fly. We can ascend to a higher view. Let's take another look—a look at the *whole* picture. Observe all our sub personalities, our bodies, and our minds all taking part in a delicate, breathtaking design—a design that flows from sound—sound that is the Divine Word made manifest.

And while we watch and hear this song of ourselves, we may also see that Great Spirit is always singing to us a slightly higher note, calling us, vibrating us, enticing us, showing us that what we thought was our chaos was instead a holy labyrinthine path that spirals finally so deep into Divinity that we can no longer cry "we're only human," for we have seen our own light.

It is in that center point of deep divinity that you find that you and God are the Ancient One. That you and the Goddess-In-All are the One who flies above your body and sings it to sleep. It is you and God-In-You, Immanuel, who is overcome with joy at the very sound of your heart beating. You, *the One, the whispering witness to all that has made your body laugh and cry*, all the while calling out comfort. "It is all right" you say to yourself. "You are sad now only because you have forgotten who you are."

Every thought you have, every move you make is sacred, because each thought and each move is carrying you deeper into mindfulness. We all have a multiple personalitied ego will which casts votes and takes action in more or less sensible ways. And we also have a higher self will which is already in harmony with Divine will. Every single happening, every dream, every meal, every pain, every joy is designed to show us how to click our ego will into gear with our interior, inherited, ingrained, implicate will that is one with the will of Perfect Love.

> *The self (Atman)...is free from evil,*
> *free from old age, free from death,*
> *free from grief, free from hunger*
> *and thirst, whose desire is real,*
> *whose thoughts are true.*
> —Chandogya Unpanishad, ancient Hindu scripture

> *Every creature participates in some*
> *way in the likeness of the Divine essence.*
> —Thomas Aquinas, 13th century Italian theologian and Catholic saint

YOU ARE JESUS

Mother Teresa said that the lepers, the poor, and the dying that she cared for were all Jesus. How could she say that? What a brilliant way to show the paradox of humanity and divinity! These human beings were ill, some so sick they could not even speak or care for themselves. They were not preaching wisdom or speaking in parables or raising people from the dead. Or were they?

What if the sight of their suffering awakens compassion in a frozen heart? Is that not a miracle of resurrection? But Mother Teresa meant even more than that. They are all Jesus simply because they are all Jesus, and in being so, it is a great privilege to be allowed to minister to them.

Just so, we, though perhaps not ill, perhaps not dying—we are all Jesus as well. Not because of what we do. *We just are.*

In addition to that, we all have 'lepers' within us—parts of us we consider untouchable and unlovable. We hide those parts of us away in dark caves and on inaccessible islands and hope they'll disappear if we just don't look at them. Mistakes we've made, lies we've told, secret shames we've hidden, memories of pain we've caused others. All of these are our lepers within. For generations, we've tried to hide them from the light of our consciousness, *not understanding that they lie in their rags and bandages waiting to heal us.*

Let us look deep into our souls. Let us look in the shadowy places for the parts of us that we thought were too ugly, too weak, too poor, and too sick to accept. Let us embrace them one by one and lead them out into the light of our mindfulness. Just as Mother Teresa would have done, let us clean the wounds of those parts of us and honor them. They are all Jesus. They are all holy, sacred, divine and one with us.

As you kneel beside them—all those neglected parts of yourself—tending to their needs; allow yourself the ecstasy, the pure joy of realizing you are being given the privilege of ministering to a great and holy one. You are being given the opportunity to care for and love the leper within you, the wounded healer within you.

It is in such work as this, as we minister to our inner selves and create a healing temple there for every sacred part of us, that we become blinded by our own light. And in that blindness—see. See, once and for all, that we are literally made of nothing less than Pure Unconditional Love. And in that seeing, understand that everyone and everything is made of us and we of them.

Your divinity is the electricity that runs through the insulated power line of your humanity and lights the world. You are heaven wrapped in earth's arms.

You are the Ancient One; of the Implicate Order of Perfection. You asked for fingers and toes so as to walk on sand and touch your lover's face.

You are Divinity Dancing in time and space.

> *Whatever is found in creatures is*
> *found in the Divine.*
> —Nicholas of Cusa, 15th century German
> philosopher and Catholic cardinal

THE CHAKRA CONNECTION:
SEVENTH BLESSING—DIVINITY
SEVENTH CHAKRA—TRANSCENDENCE

> *To know what is impenetrable to*
> *us really exists, manifesting itself to*
> *us as the highest wisdom and the*
> *most radiant beauty...This knowledge,*
> *this feeling is at the center of all*
> *true religiousness and spirituality.*
> —Albert Einstein, 20th century physicist

May you be so astonished by your own holiness that the halo emanating from your seventh chakra becomes visible to you. We began with the first chakra at the base of the spine in the first chapter and have explored the second, third, fourth, fifth, and sixth. Now we are at the top of the head, the locus of the seventh chakra. Energetically, this chakra is connected to the brain and the pineal gland. Among Hindus, this chakra is often depicted as a lotus blossom on top of the head. In Christianity saints are often depicted with halos, indicating an awareness of a special glow around the heads of those with a strong connection to God. Tongues of fire appeared on top of the heads of the apostles when they were filled with the Holy Spirit.

The seventh chakra is also often called the crown chakra, implying our connection with royalty. We each have our own crown, for we are, each one of us, divine princes and princesses, fully endowed with all the riches and the keys to the Kingdom of Adoration and Joy.

It is at this crown chakra where we are crowned and baptized and anointed. It is at the crown chakra where we intuitively sense our physical connection with the Living Water, the Burning Flame, and the Rushing Mighty Wind. The more we meditate, the more we are able to feel the heat at the top of our heads as we open the petals of the lotus blossom there for larger and larger streamings of Divinity to pour through. Those with eyes to see have witnessed the golden rays that continually shine upon each one of us, inviting us to open to the Sacred Penetration, the Divine Ecstasy.

As we grow more and more awake to who we truly are, we learn to harmonize our chakras, allowing them all to spin freely and vibrate at their own distinctive tones. This happens as we discover our true identities and lovingly embrace all of who we are—guilts, fears, tensions, pleasures, honors, secrets, heart racing passions—the whole amazing us. Then each note of us resounds in perfect pitch—all seven notes of the universal key. Then each color of us emerges in a complete chromatic spectrum—all seven colors of red, orange, yellow, green, blue, indigo, violet. Then each blessing of us begins to hum, and we, in our humble radiance, find our wings and our oneness.

May you breathe in through your crown chakra, and, as you inhale, feel the Godhead pouring the Everlasting Elixir of Light into you through the point at the top of your head. As you exhale, may you breathe out luminous color with a most harmonious hum. *Your very breathing is a song to the Earth and a symphony to Heaven.*

> His intense craving begins to pull
> at God with an irresistible force. The
> Lord as the Cosmic Vision is drawn
> by that magnetic ardor into the
> seeker's range of consciousness.

—Paramahansa Yogananda, 20th century yogi

EXPERIENCING THE BLESSING

1. Sit in a quiet place and close your eyes. With your index fingers, gently feel your face. Feel your soft skin, the fascinating rigid bridge of your nose, the wiggly cartilaginous end of your nose. Feel the sharp eyebrow ridge above your eyes, your delicate lashes, your cheekbones, the little valley at the center above your upper lip. And what a miracle is your mouth, your teeth, and tongue. What wonders come from just your mouth—words, kisses, whispers, prayers.

To do this long enough is to become struck with awe at the very *be-ing* of your amazing, sacred body. To do this long enough is to begin to find your body a most comfortable and intriguing place in which to dwell while marrying earth to heaven. While digging our toes into motherly mud, we stretch our fingers up into the raining sky.

2. This exercise I learned from human potential seminar leaders, Bob and Ann Nunley. You need a partner to do this. Sit across from one another in a peaceful place where you will not be distracted. Know that each of you has a luminous higher self or spirit, and that you are both fully capable of glimpsing this being. Look at each other with soft focus as if you are looking slightly above and around your partner yet still aware of their physical presence. Relax. Don't try to force an image. Just trust that it will come. There is no rush. Once you have received an image or an impression, share it with your partner.

This can be a very intimate and beautiful exercise with just two people and also with small groups of 5 or 6. When several people look to see one person's higher self, they often report startling similarities in what they have all seen. This is very validating for the person being observed, because there often is so much consensus about the essence of their higher self. It helps them to know their true selves much better.

3. This exercise, like most of the others, is best done when not operating heavy machinery. While you're doing something rather routine, identify with your higher self or spirit and rise up slightly above your body's head so that you can look at everything your body is looking at, only from a few inches above your physical eyes. Remind yourself that you are seeing from the perspective of your soul. You are seeing your surroundings in their true sacred radiance without the filter of the ego which evaluates things for your body's purposes. You are seeing your surroundings with the eyes of God. What glory do you see?

> *In Him we live and move and have*
> *our being...for we are indeed His offspring.*
> —Paul, Acts 17:28, Holy Bible, sacred Christian text

A PRAYER

*Oh Grace, Oh Beauty, Oh Bright
Morningstar, Oh Living Lotus*

*How can it be that You dwell and breathe
and love in us? How can it be that You
reside and move in the mountains and the
seas and in every creature and every
point and wave of energy? How can it be that
we do exist wholly and utterly within You?*

*Teach us to see. Teach us to behold You in
all our companions and all our enemies and
in each one of us.*

*Help us to gaze in the mirror and witness
the Divine Spark above our heads, behind our
eyes, glowing beneath our skin and in the
very walls around us. You it is Who guides
us ever into You-in-us and You-in-all. How
beautiful is this journey with You, oh, Gentle
Gypsy, dancing with us down the endless
road of Infinite Love.*

Omm Amen, We are One—Ho

8th

THE GATHERLING OF INFINITY

THE EMERGENCE OF THE INFINITE HUMANE

YOU ARE INFINITE

You are at once infinitely loving, powerfilled, creative, and divine. You are an eternal creature forever alive. In moments of blissful, blessingful oneness, may you see the holy perfection of 'all your relations' and of yourself. You are seven-blessed, infinitely sacred, and roundly, endlessly cherished. You are My Beloved.

The Gateway of Infinity

It is in the counting of our blessings, from one to seven, that we begin to awaken, indeed to become conscious, of who we have always been. With this awakening, a radical evolutionary leap is taking place among us. We have walked the path of the seven blessings, and they have led us here to this gateway of infinity. Let us dare to step through the portal and consciously, willingly accept ourselves fully for who we truly are.

> *Let us conquer the world with our love.*
> —Mother Teresa, 20th century spiritual leader

> *We are at the dawn of an age in*
> *which extreme political concepts and*
> *dogmas may cease to dominate*
> *human affairs. We must use this*
> *historic opportunity to replace them*
> *with universal human and spiritual values.*
> —His Holiness the Dalai Lama, 20th century
> Tibetan spiritual leader

Infinity is here—now. We are living in the cradling time of the Infinite Human, also known as Homo Novo, Homo Noeticus, the Possible Human, the Universal Human. We are moving from self-doubt to self-sanctification. We are moving from fear-based options to love as our mover and shaker.

> *Belonging to different religious tra-*
> *ditions must not constitute today a*
> *source of opposition and tension.*
> —Pope John Paul II, 20th century, Roman Catholic
> spiritual leader

We are going within and finding our sacred wholeness. When we return to our earthly tasks, we increasingly find that we have no adversaries, for the only adversary there was (which was ourselves) has been embraced.

We have loved our families fiercely, protected them, and fought for them. Now we are seeing that our family is very, very big—as big as all life, and our protective ardor is expanding to infinity.

> *The call for a worldwide fellowship*
> *that lifts neighborly concern beyond*
> *one's tribe, race, class, and nation is*
> *in reality a call for an all-embracing*
> *and unconditional love for all men.*
> *This oft misunderstood and misin-*
> *terpreted concept... has now become*
> *an absolute necessity for the survival of man.*
> —Martin Luther King, 20th century,
> spiritual and civil rights leader

> *What is happening at Black Mesa is*
> *happening all over the world. Now*
> *is the time for spiritual people to*
> *come together, to sit down, face-to-*
> *face, and unite through prayer.*
> —Thomas Banyacya, 20th century,
> Native American Hopi Elder

> *We must now progress beyond the*
> *speciesist ethic of the era of factory*
> *farming, of the use of animals as*
> *mere research tools, of whaling,*
> *seal hunting, kangaroo slaughter,*
> *and the destruction of wilderness.*
> *We must take the final step in ex-*
> *panding the circle of ethics.*
> —Peter Singer, 20th century Australian
> professor, author, and animal activist

THE EVOLUTION OF LOVE CONSCIOUSNESS

We are witnessing, right now, an evolution of consciousness. We are in the midst of a visibly evolving species—ourselves. We are experiencing the comprehension and manifestation of a new world view. We have been encoded with wings always. We have been implicate butterflies even while sometimes crawling about with eyes downcast. Now we are beginning to weave our chrysalises, and one by one we are emerging new creatures with new eyes and new visions.

Love has been building up energy for centuries. The wind has carried eons of love upon its breath. Mother Earth has sent up infinite, uncountable gifts from her body to feed, clothe, house, heal, and comfort us. We have been swimming in a Sea of Love.

By the words, thoughts, and actions of all of us and all our relations, we have given love form and increased its visibility and tangibility. We have been co-creating love with the Divine Creator on this planet for centuries. Now we are reaching a critical mass of this love. Yes, there have been wars and murders and acts of hate and destruction, but these have not halted the exponential, glacial moving-in of love.

Perhaps, this sounds a bit naive in the midst of so much global chaos and uncertainty over our technological, political, and economic capacity to survive into the 21st century. It is tempting sometimes to become pessimistic about our chances of successfully dodging all these bullets. So it helps to remember who we are and what we are capable of. We are vibratory beings, made of light. Recall the experiments that Hans Yennie did with sound frequencies applied to a tray of sand. As the vibration changed, the pattern in the sand changed. We can change our vibrations and, thus, change the pattern of things to come. As God pours through us, as we allow the Divine to speak words of beauty and harmony and love through us, we will, and already are, seeing miracles of transformation around us.

> *When, one by one, we collectively*
> *reach a critical mass in spiritual*
> *consciousness, we can make a*
> *quantum leap into a new tomorrow.*
> *This has always been the call of the mystics.*
> —Louann Stahl, 20th century American author

> *Through the silent, hidden work of*
> *the masters, men and women*
> *throughout the world are beginning*
> *to intuitively understand the truth.*
> *There is a vibration, call it the*
> *master vibration, that is flowing*
> *through the consciousness of man-*
> *kind, turning each individual*
> *toward the light within and it is*
> *only a matter of time before the dawning.*
> —John Randolph Price, 20th century American author

WE NEVER LEFT THE GARDEN

We stand today on a tectonic shift of body-mind-spirit consciousness. This earthquakian shaking up of old paradigms is unsettling and resettling. We are looking at new shorelines and new vistas as we live through this cataclysmic polar shift in human consciousness.

> *Mankind is slowly evolving towards*
> *a sublime state of consciousness of*
> *which fleeting glimpses have been*
> *afforded to us by all the great seers*
> *and mystics of the past and present.*
> —Gopi Krishna, 20th century Indian mystic

Pir-O-Murshid Inayat Khan, a 20th century Sufi mystic, came to the United States with a message some years ago. It was that God would be more and more evident in more and more beings during this century. No longer would the mystical experience be known by only a few rare yogis, shamans, avatars, and saints.

Philosophers and spiritual teachers are proposing that the purpose of our existence and our evolution is to become conscious of our divinity and out-picture it on earth; that is to co-create heaven on earth with the Creator. Christ is constantly coming again and again, visiting us, singing to us, entreating us to awaken to our true nature.

> *Run to his feet—He is standing close*
> *to your head right now. You have*
> *slept for millions and millions of*
> *years. Why not wake up this morning?*
> —Kabir, 15th century Indian mystic and poet

Many mental and physical health practitioners have opened themselves up to the spiritual nature of humanity. They have proclaimed that inner peace and well-being emanate from a conscious awareness of the sanctity of all life, including our own. Gregg Braden has pointed out that, when we shift our emotions from rage and envy to compassion, that conscious shifting activates genetic codes which then trigger an improved immune system.

Many myths from many cultures tell the story of human beings coming to earth and forgetting their divine origins, forgetting that they were part of the Infinite Whole. The story of Adam and Eve expresses this deep belief that somehow we are separate from God and, as such, must suffer on earth. But too many people, too many times, have shaken us in our slumber and yelled out with great fervor—*we are not lost, nor are we unloved, nor are we separate from God.* We never left the Garden. Let us open our sleepy eyes and see.

Many scientists are telling us now that *we are nonlocal beings, unlimited by time and space.* We are spiritual beings—much, much more than bodies, brains, and personalities.

> *For humans to be part of*
> *the peace process, to cease being*
> *warriors against Mother Earth, a*
> *great awakening must take place.*

> *That awakening, I am convinced, will*
> *be an awakening in our mystical*
> *consciousness. It is already well underway.*
> —Matthew Fox, 20th century American theologian and
> author

THE NEW "CULTURAL CREATIVES"

A social analyst, by the name of Paul Ray, recently reported that the fastest growing subculture in the U.S., nearly 25% of adult Americans, is made up of what he calls "cultural creatives". These are people who value living with respect for all life. They see the value of integrating body, mind, and spirit; of respecting the environment, all species, all ages, all cultures and religions. They are moving in the direction of living from their higher altruistic, spiritually committed selves, healing and transforming the world before it is destroyed. They share a belief that humanity is basically loving. They are coming to understand what the new scientists are teaching: that consciousness is causal. These cultural creatives believe that we can consciously choose how we want to evolve our bodies and our consciousness, and that *we are fully capable of choosing to evolve our species in the direction of higher love and full awareness of our intense connectivity with all life.*

HOPE ON THE HORIZON

We are beginning to comprehend the nature of matter, how the brain works, and how our bodies work. We are inventing technology that is growing so exponentially that solutions to many problems are not far away. Energy researchers report to us that, until recently, energy technology has been based on the concept of entropy. We had to destroy something (for example, coal and air quality) to create power. Now we are moving toward the science of the creative inward spiral which produces decentralized, nondestructive forms of energy for fuel, electricity, and heat. Renewable, nonpolluting energy technology is no longer just an idealistic fantasy.

Add to that the fact that there is a huge burgeoning multitude of cultural creatives reaching their retirement years when they can throw enormous amounts of time and talent and heart into this spiritual awakening and evolution. In addition to that the Internet is granting, heretofore, unheard of power to people for grass roots networking and combining forces.

Barbara Marx Hubbard proposes a new model for consciously evolving ourselves and society. She wants to develop "Peace Rooms" which use advanced communication technology, like the Internet, to find out what is working all over the world to solve hunger, poverty, pollution, and other problems, so that we can build on what already works.

FINCA (Foundation for International Community Assistance) and other microloan groups are perfect examples of grass roots organizations that work. FINCA alone has loaned millions of dollars in tiny $50.00 and $100.00 loans to enterprising, yet poverty stricken, women to start businesses of their own. This worldwide micro loan program is so successful, that the optimistically possible prediction is that hunger and poverty will be unknown by the year 2020.

We who have had food and shelter long enough can now reach inside us and see what else is there. And it is beautiful what we have found. We are finding that if we follow our bliss, we will soon find the gifts we came to give. And if we speak these gifts out loud, we will see how they fit into this great cosmic shift in our evolution; we will see how we came to bring more love to the world.

People magazine recently ran an article about a large group of newly very rich young people who are retiring early from their corporate jobs and developing self-sustaining foundations to help others. Scott Oki, a former Microsoft employee, says of his fellow givers: "We have yet to see the tidal wave of what these Microsoft people will do 10, 20, 30 years from now. It's going to be huge."

GLOBAL PEACE AND A SUSTAINABLE EARTH

Willis Harman and Howard Rheingold , in their book *Higher Creativity* tell us that: "Collectively held unconscious beliefs are the most fundamental cause of the dilemmas that beset the world today." But these beliefs can change, and they are changing. Because of that, Willis and Howard say, "the achievement of global peace and a sustainable planetary society is feasible..."

We are the bearers of a new vision.
We can dispel the old destructive
myths and replace them with life
enriching truths that are essential
to continued life on our planet.
—Ken Keyes. 20th century American author

Rest in peace, for we shall not repeat the sin.
—Inscription to the victims on the Hiroshima
Peace Park Memorial

In September of 1997, the Global Futures Foundation hosted an Ecotech Conference in California. It was attended by activists and visionaries, engineers and scientists, and corporate leaders. All these diverse people came together in "a spirit of collaboration and synergy" to create "products, processes, and organizations that are good for people, business, and the planet." They discussed doing business with "choardic alliance principles" (from "chaos" and "order") which were partly inspired by the Alcoholics Anonymous model of operating without structure but with direction. The "partnership model" of business was shared. Others brainstormed over ways to preserve biodiversity and to integrate environmental priorities into long-term business strategies.

When we greet the unexpected with
enthusiasm—that is, with faith in
"God within"—we will find answers
that go beyond any of our own imaginings.
—Barbara Bartocci, 20th century American author

Let us pray with thousands of others each day the prayer initiated by Masahisa Goi—"May Peace Prevail on Earth." After witnessing the horrors of World War II, Mr. Goi wanted to find a way to help people focus on peace. In 1955, he founded the World Peace Prayer Society. In 1990, the Society was officially recognized by the United Nations as a non-governmental organization. Many people have dedicated themselves to repeating this universal prayer every day at noon. Think of the vibratory power of all those prayers to lift us all to a higher consciousness of compassion, love, and harmlessness.

SEVEN BLESSINGS FOR SEVEN GENERATIONS INFINITE LOVE FOR ALL-THAT-IS

There is blessed hope on the horizon for this sacred planet and for life. We are wonder workers—you and I. We are blessed seven times over and infinitely so. Native Americans teach us that we must choose our actions based on how they will affect our children seven generations from now. May our blessings be their blessings. May we: the Seven-Times-Blessed Infinite Humans prepare a sustainable earth and a broad, encompassing circle of compassion that embraces all living creatures and all creation. May we create a world at peace, a world of reverence and love for:

all the beings who
ever come, with hope in their eyes,
to live and love on this beautiful
blue-green planet home of ours.

Let us see how we can, with our Seven Blessings, make Infinite Love.

Epilogue
Compassion In Action:
Holding The Vision Of Peace On Earth

I thank you all for reading this book. I pray that it has been inspiring to each one of you. I sense that many of you are already very active in bringing about peace and compassion among your families and, perhaps, within your communities or even on a global scale. However, you and I know many people who have not yet caught the vision of this emerging spiritual consciousness that we are witnessing. The simplest way I've found to understand this emerging consciousness is that, as we gain in spiritual awareness, we experience less and less fear and move toward more and more love. Many people on the planet are still living in a great deal of fear, more fear than is necessary for survival; and that fear causes great suffering. All of these folks are blessed as we are; all are sacred beings, yet they remain unaware of their Divine origins.

Some of these people are extremely powerful and are making daily decisions which affect large numbers of beings and the earth as well. There are corporate leaders in the lumber industry, agribusiness, energy and oil companies, pharmaceutical companies, and many other businesses who literally have the power to save vast acres of rain forest, stop the suffering of millions of animals and people, stop significant amounts of pollution, and stop destroying the homes and cultures of indigenous people. They have the power to reverse the trend of destruction and invest in sustainable and compassionate business practices which will benefit future generations globally, rather than just a few people today.

Gandhi and Schweitzer and many other spiritual giants have made it clear that we will not evolve as spiritually conscious human beings nor will we be able to create world peace if we do not have compassion and reverence for all beings, human and otherwise.

There are many leaders in government, including dictators who promote hatred and fear, as well as politicians who use their power primarily for personal gain. These are all brilliant, powerful, ambitious, extremely intelligent men and women. Imagine what would happen if they could catch the vision of a world at peace; if they could replace their fear with love and compassion. If they could be lifted up enough to see that they are one with us and we with them; and that, what they do to the earth and the beings of earth, they do to themselves—imagine the results. If they could adopt the highest ethic that befits the level of their power and lend their strength to solving the world's challenges of hunger, pollution, crime, war, poverty, and cruelty— imagine the power of that.

I am certainly not suggesting that all politicians, corporate leaders, and wealthy people are driven by fear and abuse their power. In ever increasing numbers, many are making wise and caring decisions as well as donating massive amounts of money to important causes. This, in fact, gives us further indication that we are evolving to higher ethics and ideals as a species. Nevertheless, there are many others who have not yet glimpsed their true spiritual nature and their interrelationship with all creation. Because of that, they live in constant fear: fear of change, fear of loss of power and money, fear of loss of freedom, and fear of being controlled by others. In truth and in God's eyes, these people are certainly not our enemies. They are our brothers and sisters. As James Redfield says in *The Tenth Insight*, "We must uplift everyone, help them to remember, treat no one as an enemy...we must hold this vision to save the world."

In light of all this, I have a proposal to make. If you feel so moved in spirit to do so, I would like to ask you to sign the Compassion Commitment statement below and then send it to as many people in powerful, influential positions as possible. If you know them personally, a cover letter from you would give the statement more impact. If you belong to a civic group, church, charity, or other organization that would endorse this Compassion Commitment, ask them to sign on as well before sending it. Of course, if you prefer not to send it to anyone and you just want to sign it yourself, please do so and forward it on to me. Feel free to make copies of the commitment and pass them around.

If it seems appropriate to you, include a copy of this book with your signed commitment. By sending along a copy of *Born to Be Blessed,* you will be emphasizing the fact that you are not approaching these individuals in an antagonistic or polarizing manner. You are, instead, reminding them of their true and sacred nature and inviting them to journey on with us into this breathtaking quantum leap in spiritual consciousness that we are taking as we enter the new millennium.

I can hear some of you more practical readers sounding the alarm that such a move as this is futile and naive. Whenever we take these kinds of actions, *it is very important to remember who we are. We are God's miracle workers,* and we are working with the Power of God's Love. When we join together to hold a vision for global peace, sustainability, and universal compassion for all beings, we are aligning ourselves and getting in synch with God's Infinite Power and our own divinity. Even if you get no personal response from your letters, even if you see no direct physical results from your actions, know this: *that everything you do in the name of Love makes a difference. Everything you do to bring more Compassion to earth, no matter how small it may seem to you, has a profound and everlasting effect on all Creation.*

THE COMPASSION COMMITMENT

HOLDING THE VISION FOR A WORLD ENCIRCLED WITH PEACE AND LOVE

Until we extend our circle of compassion to include all living things, we will not ourselves find peace.
Albert Schweitzer (paraphrased)

WE, the human residents of this beautiful, blue-green Planet Earth, do hereby declare that all of creation is sacred and interconnected. We know that all the stones, the mountains, the trees, the birds, the fish, the bears, the wind, the sun, all-that-is and we, ourselves, are worthy of awe and wonder. Whatever happens to one of us, happens to us all. We understand that the Divine Creator is Love and exists in everything, everywhere, making every being an embodiment of Divine Love.

WE recognize that we can choose to evolve in the direction of full spiritual consciousness. We are spiritual beings blessed with eternal oneness, power, love, creativity, perfection, and divinity. We are rising from the status of competitive survivors to becoming gentle, compassionate caretakers of this miracle known as Planet Earth. We are expanding our circle of compassion to include all of God's creation, the entire family of earth.

WE hold the vision that, with God's unfailing Love and Assistance, we can create a world free of hunger and poverty and prejudice; a world free of war and violence against the earth, against animals, and against human beings; a world free of hatred and fear.

WE will use our power in our roles as parents, teachers, investors, consumers, voters, and active participants in life to promote harmlessness and compassion for all beings, peace and justice, environmental sustainability, and to do our part to help life evolve to its full flowering in spiritual consciousness. In Mother Teresa's words, "Let us conquer the world with our love."

WE commit ourselves to hold this vision close to our hearts and to pray this prayer:

> *Oh, Divine One, we give thanks continually to You for loving us so completely and, thereby, showing us how to encircle the earth with Love and Compassion as you encircle us. May Love, Peace, and Compassion for all Beings be expressed everywhere on earth. Amen*

Postscript from Judy: Blessings and thanks to you all for reading *Born to Be Blessed* and the Compassion Commitment statement. A portion of the profits from this book will be donated to charities that promote human and animal rights, peace and justice work, and environmental causes.

Select Bibliography

Abell, Arthur. *Talks with Great Composers.* Lakeside, CA: Psychic Book Club, 1955.

Aurobindo, Sri. *Savitri: A Legend and a Symbol.* Pondicherry, India: Ashram Press, 1948.

Bach, Richard. *Jonathan Livingston Seagull.* New York: Avon, 1973.

Bartocci, Barbara. *Unexpected Answers.* Huntington, Indiana: Our Sunday Visitor, 1994.

Black Elk, Wallace and Lyon, William S. *Black Elk: The Sacred Ways of a Lakota.* New York: Harper and Row, 1990.

Blakney, R.B. *The Way of Life: Lao Tzu. Tao Te Ching: A New Translation by R.B. Blakney.* New York: Mentor Books, 1964.

Bohm, David. *Wholeness and the Implicate Order.* New York, NY: Routledge and Kegan Paul, 1980.

Boom, Corrie ten, with Sherrill, John and Sherrill, Elizabeth. *The Hiding Place.* Washington Depot, Connecticut: Chosen Books, 1971.

Braden, Gregg. *Walking Between the Worlds: The Science of Compassion.* Radio Bookstore Press, 1997.

Bradshaw, John. *Creating Love: The Next Great Stage of Growth.* New York: Bantam Books, 1992.

Brand, Paul and Yancey, Philip. *Fearfully and Wonderfully Made: A Surgeon Looks at the Human and Spiritual Body.* Grand Rapids, Michigan: Zondervan Publishing House, 1980.

Brown, Joseph Epes, Ed. *Black Elk: The Sacred Pipe.* New York, NY: Penguin Books, 1987.

Brunsting, Bernard. (Einstein's letter) "The Difference You Can Make," Pawling, NY: Plus: *The Magazine for Positive Living.* May, 1987.

Cerminara, Gina. *Many Mansions: "The Edgar Cayce Story on Reincarnation".* New York: New American Library, 1967.

Clarke, Richard (translator). "Verses on the Faith-Mind by Sengstan." Buffalo, New York: White Pine Press, 1984.

Colijn, Helen. *Song of Survival.* Ashland, Oregon: White Cloud Press, 1995.

Dass, Ram, in collaboration with Stephen Levine. *Grist for the Mill.* Santa Cruz, CA: Unity Press, 1977.

Daya Mata. *God Alone.* Los Angeles, CA: Self Realization Fellowship.

de Foucauld, Charles. *Spiritual Autobiography of Charles de Foucauld.* Denville, NJ: Dimension Books, 1964.

Dossey, Larry. *Space, Time, and Medicine.* Boston: New Science Library, 1982. And Recovering the Soul: A Scientific and Spiritual Search. New York: Bantam Books, 1989.

Dyer, Wayne. *The Sky's the Limit.* New York: Simon and Schuster, 1980.

Emerson, Ralph Waldo. (Edward Waldo Emerson, Ed.) *The Complete Works of Ralph Waldo Emerson.* Boston, Mass.:Houghton Mifflin.

Fox, Matthew. *Breakthrough: Meister Eckhart's Creation Spirituality in New Translation.* Garden City, NY: Doubleday and Co., 1980.

Fox, Matthew. *The Coming of the Cosmic Christ.* San Francisco: Harper and Row, 1988.

Fox, Matthew, Ed. *Hildegard of Bingen's Book of Divine Works, with Letters and Songs.* Santa Fe, NM: Bear and Co., 1987.

Fox, Matthew. *Meditations with Meister Eckhart.* Santa Fe, NM: Bear and Co., 1982.

Gibran, Khalil. *The Prophet.* New York: Knopf, 1952.

Hamilton, Michelle with Rachelle Hamilton. "Swept to Sea," *Readers' Digest* (August, 1992).

Harman, Willis and Rheingold, Howard: *Higher Creativity: Liberating the Unconscious for Breakthrough Insights.* Los Angeles, CA: Jeremy Tarcher, Inc., 1984.

Houston, Jean. *The Possible Human: A Course in Enhancing Your Physical, Emotional, and Creative Abilities.* New York: Jeremy P. Tarcher, 1982.

Hubbard, Barbara Marx. *The Revelation: A Message of Hope for the New Millennium*. Mill Valley, CA: Natara, 1995.

Huxley, Aldous. *The Doors of Perception*. New York, NY: HarperCollins Publishers, 1963.

Jacobson, Simon. *The Wisdom of the Rebbe Manachem Mendel Schneerson*. New York: William Morrow and Co., 1995.

Johnston, William (ed.). *The Cloud of Unknowing and the Book of Privy Counseling: An Enduring Classic of Christian Mystical Experience*. Garden City, NY: Image Books, 1973.

Kearney, Jack. "Father's Great Expectations," Carmel, NY: *Guideposts Magazine*. August, 1993.

Keyes, Ken Jr. *The Hundredth Monkey*. Coos Bay, OR: Vision Books, 1983.

Khan, Pir Vilayat Inayat. *The Message in Our Time: The Life and Teaching of the Sufi Master Pir-O-Murshid Inayat Khan*. New York: Harper and Row, 1978.

King Jr., Martin Luther. (Coretta Scott King, designer, James M. Washington, Ed.) *I Have a Dream: Writings and Speeches That Changed the World by Martin Luther King*. San Francisco, CA: Harper, 1992.

King, Ursula. *Towards a New Mysticism: Teilhard de Chardin and Eastern Religions*. New York, NY: Seabury Press, 1980.

Krishna, Gopi. *The Biological Basis of Religion and Genius*. New York: Harper and Row, 1972.

Kushner, Rabbi Harold. *When All You've Ever Wanted Isn't Enough*. New York: NY: Summit Books, Simon and Schuster, 1986.

McLaughlin, John. "Within You Without You: The Guitarist's Search for Spiritual Meaning." *Guitar Player Magazine*, May, 1995.

Moody, Raymond A. *Life After Life*. New York: Bantam Books, 1975.

Moore, Thomas. *Soul Mates: Honoring the Mysteries of Love and Relationship*. New York: Harper Collins, 1994.

Myss, Caroline. *Anatomy of the Spirit: The Seven Stages of Power and Healing.* New York: Harmony Books, 1996.

Norris, Kathleen. *The Cloister Walk.* Riverhead Books, 1996.

Nunley, Ann Pierce. *Inner Counselor: An Intuitive Guide for Life's Journey.* Pittsburgh, PA: SterlingHouse Publishers, 1999.

O'Neal, David (ed.). *Meister Eckhart, from whom God Hid Nothing: Sermons, Writings, and Sayings.* Boston: Shambhala, 1996.

Oyle, Irving. *Time, Space, and the Mind.* Millbrae, CA: Celestial Arts, 1976.

Patent, Arnold. *You Can Have It All: The Art of Winning the Money Game and Living a Life of Joy.* Piermont, New York: Money Mastery Publishing, 1987.

Peace Pilgrim. *Steps Toward Inner Peace: Harmonious Principles for Human Living by Peace Pilgrim.* Santa Fe, NM: Ocean Tree Books, 1986.

Peale, Norman Vincent. "The Blessed Assurance," *Life After Death.* Carmel, NY: Guide-posts, 1987.

Perkins, John. *The World Is As You Dream It: Shamanic Teachings From the Amazon and Andes.* Rochester, VT, 1994.

Plummer, William and Kelley, Tina. "The Givers," *People Magazine.* (October 27, 1997).

Price, John. *The Superbeings.* New York: Ballantine Books, 1981.

Richards, M.C. *Imagine Inventing Yellow: New and Selected Poems of M.C. Richards.* Barrytown, NY: Barrytown Ltd., 1997.

Rilke, Rainer Maria. (Stephen Mitchell, Trans.) *The Selected Poetry of Rainer Maria Rilke.* New York, NY: Vintage Books, 1984.

Ritchie, George C. "Return from Tomorrow," *Life After Death.* Carmel, N.Y.: Guideposts, 1987.

Roberts, Jesse. "Lost in the Fiji Islands," *Guideposts Magazine.* (December, 1996).

Ross, Michael. "The Urge to Hurt," *Utne Reader*. (July-August, 1997).

Ruopp, Julia Phillips. "The Window of Heaven," *Life After Death*. Carmel, N.Y.: Guideposts, 1987.

Siegel, Bernie. *Love, Medicine, and Miracles*. New York: Harper and Row, 1986.

Singer, Peter. *Animal Liberation: A New Ethics For Our Treatment of Animals*. New York: Avon Books, 1975.

Stahl, Louann. *A Most Surprising Song: Exploring the Mystical Experience*. Unity Village, MO: Unity Books, 1992.

Sudo, Philip Toshio. *Zen Guitar*. New York: Simon and Schuster, 1997.

Swinney, Mark. "Deliver Us From Evil," *The Christian Science Journal*. April, 1996.

Talbot, Michael. *The Holographic Universe*. New York: HarperCollins, 1991.

Teresa, Mother. (Gonzalez-Balado, Jose Luis, Ed.) *Heart of Joy*. Ann Arbor, Michigan: Servant Books, 1987.

Thesenga, Susan. *The Undefended Self: Living the Pathwork of Spiritual Wholeness*. Based on the Pathwork material created by Eva Pierrakos. Madison, VA: Pathwork Press, 1994.

Thich Nhat Hanh. *Peace is Every Step: The Path of Mindfulness in Everyday Life*. New York, NY: Bantam Books, 1992.

Thomas, Lewis. *The Lives of a Cell*. New York, NY: Penguin, USA, 1995.

Thurman, Howard (selected by Anne Spencer Thurman). *Howard Thurman: For the Inward Journey: The Writings of Howard Thurman*. Richmond, Indiana: Friends United Meeting, 1984.

Trevelyan, Katharine. *Through Mine Own Eyes*. New York: NY: Holt, Rinehart, and Winston, 1962.

Whitman, Walt. *Leaves of Grass*. New York: Aventine Press, 1931.

Wijngaards, John. *Experiencing Jesus: Scripture, the Witness of Saints and Mystics, and a Life of Prayer Show the Way*. Notre Dame, Indiana: Ave Maria Press, 1981.

Wolf, Fred Alan. *Parallel Universes: The Search for Other Worlds*. New York: Simon and Schuster, 1988.

Woodman, Marion and Bly, Robert. "Bly and Woodman on Men and Women." Set of six video tapes. Belleville, Ontario: Applewood Communications, 1992.

Woodruff, Sue. *Meditations with Mechtild of Magdeburg*. Santa Fe, NM: Bear and Co., 1982.

Yockey, James Francis. *Meditations with Nicholas of Cusa*. Santa Fe, NM: Bear and Co., 1987.

Yogananda, Paramahansa. *Autobiography of a Yogi*. Los Angeles, CA: Self-Realization Fellowship, 1946.

Zimmerman, Michael. "We Need New Myths," *In Context*, (No. 20).